The Curious Kid's Guide To

HEROES & VILLAINS
OF THE BIBLE

WRITTEN BY
LAURA SMITH AND DOUG POWELL

HERO

VILLAIN

★ Prince, shepherd, prophet, priest
★ Leader of the Israelites
★ Brother of Aaron and Miriam

WORTHY®
kids

Table of
Heroes and Villains

CAIN

Genesis 4

CAIN was the firstborn child of Adam and Eve. Cain became angry and jealous of his younger brother, Abel, and took out his anger in the worst way.

☆ **Son of Adam and Eve**
☆ **First baby born**
☆ **Brother of Abel and Seth**
☆ **Farmer**

Cain was a farmer. He gave God some of the food he had grown as a gift, an offering.

Abel, a shepherd, gave God his best lambs. God liked Abel's gift, but he didn't accept Cain's gift.

ANGER ISSUES

This made Cain angry. God told Cain not to be mad but instead to do what was right. God warned Cain that if he stayed angry, he would make things worse. But Cain didn't listen. Then he called his brother Abel out into the field, and he killed Abel!

DID YOU KNOW?

Cain was jealous of his brother Abel. Joseph's brothers were also jealous of him (Genesis 37). David's brothers were jealous of him too (1 Samuel 17). Being jealous of your siblings is never a good thing.

LIAR! LIAR!

When God asked Cain where Abel was, Cain lied and answered, "I don't know." But God knew what Cain had done.

PUNISHMENT AND PROTECTION

God punished Cain by sending him away from the place where he had been born. He told Cain that no matter how hard he worked, the land would no longer grow food for him.

Even though God was angry with Cain for killing Abel and lying, God put a mark on Cain that would always protect him. Cain's anger caused him to be the first person to ever kill another person and to spend the rest of his life wandering the earth.

Q: When your parents correct you, do you get angry or do you say you're sorry and try to fix your mistakes?

NOAH

Genesis 6–9

HERO

★ Shipbuilder
★ Farmer
★ Father of Ham, Shem, and Japheth

NOAH was a good man and obeyed God even when no one else did, even when everyone around him was doing bad things.

God was sad and angry about how evil everyone on earth had become. God decided to send a giant flood to make the world new again. He told Noah he would save Noah and his family.

BUILD A BOAT

God told Noah to build a giant boat, an ark. This may have seemed foolish, since there was no rain. But God told Noah exactly how to build the ark— what size to make it, what wood to use, and how to design it—and Noah followed all of God's instructions. He spent many years building the ark—because God told him to.

The dove came back to Noah with an olive leaf, so he knew that the ground was almost dry.

ALL ABOARD!

Then God told Noah to bring his wife, his sons, their wives, and two of every kind of animal onto the boat with him. Noah obeyed.

DID YOU KNOW?

The ark was made of cypress wood and covered with pitch— a glue-like substance that is waterproof. The ark was as tall as a four-story building and as long as one and a half football fields! It had a roof with an opening below. The ark had a door on the side and three decks.

THE FLOOD

Rain fell for forty days and forty nights, and the earth
was covered with water. After 150 days, the floodwaters
began to go down. Months later, the ark touched ground
on the mountains of Ararat. Can you imagine being in a
boat with all those animals for months and months? Noah
and his family must have been eager to be on dry land,
but Noah waited until God told him it was time to get
out of the boat.

DRY LAND

When God said it was time, Noah, his family, and the
animals went out onto the dry land. Noah was grateful
to God for keeping him and his family safe.

AFTER THE FLOOD

Noah was obedient to God. He did exactly as God said. After the flood, Noah farmed
the land with his family and lived hundreds more years. Noah saved humankind by
listening to God, even when it didn't seem to make sense. God blessed Noah and his sons,
saying to them, "Be fruitful and multiply, and fill the earth."

ABRAHAM

Genesis 12–25

HERO

ABRAM, later called Abraham, was obedient to God. Throughout his life, when God asked him to do something, even when it was extremely difficult, Abraham did it. God rewarded Abraham's faithfulness.

☆ **Father of Nations**
☆ **Husband of Sarah**
☆ **Sons: Ishmael and Isaac**

God told Abram, "Leave your country and go where I tell you." So Abram left his family, his friends, and everything he knew and went where God told him to go. He took with him his wife, Sarai, and his nephew Lot.

Travelers in Bible times often used camels.

STARS IN THE SKY

God told Abram, "I will give you as many children, grandchildren, and descendants as there are stars in the sky." Abram was an old man and didn't have any children, but he believed God. God also promised Abram he would give him the land of Canaan. God promised these things to Abram with an official promise called a *covenant*. As a symbol of this covenant, God changed Abram's name to Abraham, which means "father of many."

DID YOU KNOW?

Just like God asked Abram to leave his homeland and everybody he knew, Ruth left her family and home to go to Bethlehem with Naomi.

DO I HAVE TO?

When Abraham finally had the son God had promised, God asked Abraham to take the boy, Isaac, to a mountain and give him to God as a gift, a burnt offering. Abraham had wanted children for a long time. God had given him Isaac and promised Abraham that he would have a large family. Abraham didn't want to kill his son, but he wanted to obey God. So, Abraham gathered his son, Isaac, and started up the mountain.

THE RAM

Just before Abraham sacrificed his son, God sent an angel to stop him. The angel said, "Don't hurt him. I now know how much you respect God." Isaac was safe. Abraham praised God and offered him a gift of a ram instead.

BLESSINGS

Abraham followed God throughout his life. God promised to bless and be with Abraham and his family always.

The Life & Journey of Abraham

1. *Abraham leaves Ur*
2. *Abraham travels through Babylon*
3. *Abraham called by God in Haran*
4. *Abraham arrives in the Promised Land, Shechem*
5. *Abraham moves to Egypt*
6. *Abraham returns to the Promised Land, Hebron*

SARAH

Genesis 12, 16, 18, 21, 23

HERO

★ Wife and Mother
★ Household Manager
★ Married to Abraham
★ Mother of Isaac

SARAH was loyal to her husband, Abraham, and to God. She left everything she knew to travel with Abraham to Canaan as God had instructed them to do.

God promised Sarah she would have a son. Sarah was eager to have a baby. She waited and waited, but she started to doubt God's promise to her.

IT'S DIFFICULT TO WAIT

Sarah became jealous of her servant, Hagar, who had a son named Ishmael. Sarah wanted a son of her own! But God told her to trust him and his plans. Sarah was ninety years old when God sent her a son, named Isaac, just as he had promised.

HAPPY ENDINGS

Sarah was filled with happiness and said, "God has brought me laughter!" Sarah lived to be 127 years old.

Sarah was very old when God blessed her with a baby.

DID YOU KNOW?

Just as he had changed Abraham's name, God also changed Sarah's name from Sarai to Sarah. Both Sarai and Sarah mean "princess." God changed Sarah's name when he promised her a son.

JOB

The Book of Job

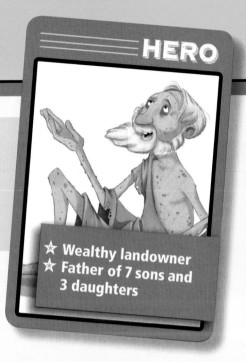

HERO

★ **Wealthy landowner**
★ **Father of 7 sons and 3 daughters**

JOB was a good man. He made virtuous choices and thanked God for everything he had. Job was also the richest man around. Even when his circumstances changed, Job remained faithful to God.

Satan saw how upright and kind Job was. Satan told God the only reason Job was so good was because he had everything he wanted. God stood up for Job. He told Satan, Job was honorable, believed in God, and turned away from evil. God told Satan he could not kill Job.

THE BAD LIFE

Satan took away Job's servants and animals. He killed Job's children. Still, Job praised God. Then Satan took away Job's health and made him very sick. Still, Job praised God. Job's three friends said Job must have done something wrong to deserve what happened to him. But still, Job trusted God.

GOD'S REMINDER

God reminded Job that he controls snow and hail and where the stars sit in the sky. Job responded, "I know you can do all things, LORD. You are more wonderful than I can ever know!"

THE GOOD LIFE, PART 2

In the end, God rewarded Job's faithfulness. He made Job healthy again and gave him a new family and twice as many riches as he had before. Job lived another 140 years.

Even though Satan took everything from Job, his belief in God remained.

ISAAC

Genesis 21–22, 24–28

ISAAC grew up in the land of Canaan, the land God had promised to his father, Abraham. Isaac received the same blessing God had given his father. Isaac obeyed his father, trusting Abraham and trusting God.

Abraham wanted Isaac to get married, so he sent his servant to their homeland to find Isaac the perfect wife. Abraham's servant brought back Rebekah. Isaac trusted Abraham's choice for him. Isaac fell in love with and married Rebekah. They had twin boys, Jacob and Esau.

BLESSED LIFE

Isaac obeyed God, and God rewarded him with blessings of flourishing crops and livestock.

OBEYING GOD

When God told Isaac to move, he took his family and his animals and moved. When God told Isaac to stay put, Isaac and his family and animals stayed. When God told Isaac to dig a well, he dug a well. Wherever Isaac and his family went, God provided food and water for them.

DID YOU KNOW?

Isaac was born when his mother, Sarah, was ninety and his father, Abraham, was 100!

JACOB

Genesis 25, 27–32

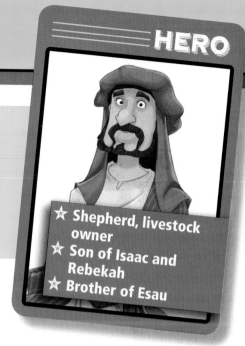

HERO

JACOB wanted the blessings God had promised. But things didn't always come easily to him. Jacob had to work and wait throughout his life. Jacob also made mistakes, like being dishonest to his father. Still God blessed Jacob in wonderful ways.

★ Shepherd, livestock owner
★ Son of Isaac and Rebekah
★ Brother of Esau

When Jacob's father, Isaac, was old, dying, and couldn't see well, Jacob and his mother came up with a scheme to acquire the inheritance that should have gone to his brother, Esau. Jacob dressed up like Esau and told his father that he was Esau. Isaac believed Jacob's lie and gave Jacob his blessing, including the land, animals, and riches that should have gone to Esau.

STAIRWAY TO HEAVEN

Jacob traveled east to avoid Esau's anger. One night, Jacob dreamed of a stairway leading to heaven. In the dream, God told Jacob he would bless Jacob with all of the descendants, riches, and blessings he had promised Abraham. Jacob praised God, promised to follow him, and made a monument to mark the place.

SUCCESS FROM GOD

Jacob tricked his own father to gain an inheritance and fled his homeland to avoid the consequences of his lie. But when Jacob fully realized how mighty the LORD was, he dedicated his life to him. Jacob's animals and crops grew, and he had a large, prosperous family, just as God had promised. Jacob gave God the glory for these blessings.

Jacob's dream of a stairway leading to heaven.

JOSEPH

Genesis 37, 39–50

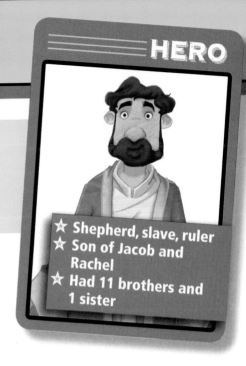

HERO

☆ Shepherd, slave, ruler
☆ Son of Jacob and Rachel
☆ Had 11 brothers and 1 sister

JOSEPH had a difficult life. He was betrayed by his brothers, sold as a slave, and sent to jail. But through it all, Joseph trusted God—and God never left his side.

Joseph's older brothers were so jealous of how much their father, Jacob, loved Joseph that they decided to get rid of him. They beat up Joseph and sold him as a slave. The slave traders carried Joseph far away to Egypt.

POTIPHAR

Even in this scary situation, Joseph honored God and God blessed Joseph. Joseph's Egyptian master, Potiphar, was pleased with Joseph's work and put Joseph in charge of everything he owned.

Ancient iron shackles, used to chain slaves

FALSELY ACCUSED

Potiphar's wife (p. 16) blamed Joseph for something he didn't do and had him thrown in jail even though he was innocent. God was with Joseph, showed him kindness, and was faithful to him while he was in prison.

TELL ME ABOUT YOUR DREAM

Years later, Pharaoh needed help interpreting a dream. Pharaoh had heard that Joseph could interpret dreams and called for him. Joseph knew that only God could understand the dream and told Pharaoh what God had revealed. Joseph told Pharaoh the dream meant a famine was coming, a time when there would be little food or water.

FOOD IN A FAMINE

Joseph helped Pharaoh save up food to prepare for the hard times ahead. When the famine came, Egypt was able to eat because of Joseph. Pharaoh rewarded Joseph and made him a ruler over the whole land of Egypt.

REMEMBER THOSE BROTHERS

Because of the famine, Joseph's brothers were starving in their land. They traveled to Egypt in hopes of getting food. Even though Joseph's brothers had been cruel, Joseph understood that it was God who sent him to Egypt, to help with the famine, so his own family could live.

FORGIVING THE FAMILY

Joseph forgave his brothers. He brought them and his father, Jacob, to live with him in Egypt, where they would always have plenty of food and water and where they could be together.

FAITHFULNESS

Throughout all the hard times, Joseph saw God working in his life. He stayed faithful to God, and God blessed him.

POTIPHAR'S WIFE

Genesis 39

POTIPHAR was a man of power and importance in Egypt. His wife caused much trouble for Joseph after Potiphar put him in charge of the household.

Potiphar's wife thought Joseph was handsome. She wanted him to like her too. But Joseph knew better. She was married to Potiphar! And Potiphar was his boss. But mostly Joseph didn't want to disobey God. Joseph asked Potiphar's wife, "How can I do this wicked thing and sin against God?" But Potiphar's wife kept trying to get Joseph to like her. And every day, Joseph said, "No."

TAKING THINGS TOO FAR

One day Potiphar's wife grabbed Joseph. Joseph ran away from her. She was mad and embarrassed that Joseph didn't like her back. She lied and told everyone Joseph had attacked her.

IT WASN'T HIS FAULT

Although Potiphar had given Joseph power over his property, Joseph was still Potiphar's slave. Potiphar believed his wife and put Joseph in jail (pp. 14–15).

IT WAS HER FAULT

Potiphar's wife lied to her husband. She didn't care about what would happen to Joseph. But God knew Joseph was innocent and would take care of him.

PHARAOH
(AT TIME OF MOSES'S BIRTH)
Exodus 1–2

VILLAIN

☆ King of Egypt
☆ Ruled at time of Moses's birth

PHARAOH was a rich and powerful king over all of Egypt. He used his thousands of Israelite slaves to build an even bigger, more magnificent kingdom. Pharaoh would stop at nothing to maintain his power over his slaves.

Pharaoh made his slaves build the cities of Pithom and Rameses. He forced them to make bricks by hand out of mud and straw. But Pharaoh felt threatened by how many Israelites there were. And even though Pharaoh treated his slaves horribly, more and more Israelites kept being born. He worried they might stand up against him or leave Egypt.

STOPPING AT NOTHING

To try to keep control, Pharaoh ordered that all Israelite baby boys be killed, believing this would lessen the number of Israelites. But the midwives—the women who helped Israelite women have their babies—would not kill the babies. They feared God and honored him. Pharaoh did terrible, desperate things to try and guard his kingdom, but the Israelites would soon be freed from Pharaoh's rule.

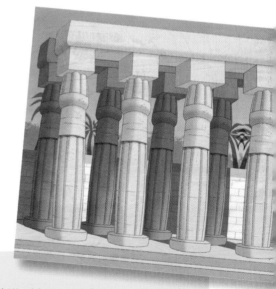

DID YOU KNOW?

Pharaoh ordered the Israelite baby boys be killed because he was worried about staying in power. Another king in the Bible did the same thing. At the time when Jesus was born, King Herod ordered all baby boys be killed because he was afraid the Messiah would be born and take Herod's throne.

JOCHEBED

Exodus 2, 6; Numbers 26

HERO

★ Mother
★ Slave
★ Children: Moses, Aaron, and Miriam

JOCHEBED was an Israelite woman living in Egypt. This meant she and her family were Pharaoh's slaves. Even though Pharaoh's law said her baby boy must die, Jochebed did all she could to protect him.

Jochebed came up with a plan to save her baby. She took a basket woven out of papyrus and waterproofed it by covering it in pitch, a tarlike substance. She placed her baby boy, Moses (pp. 22–23), in the basket and hid it in the tall grasslike reeds that grew along the Nile River, near where she lived. Jochebed asked her daughter, Miriam (p. 26), to watch the baby from a distance.

WORTH IT!

Saving her baby was dangerous. Jochebed could be killed for breaking Pharaoh's law. But she loved her son and would do anything to save him.

DID YOU KNOW?

The Pharaoh's daughter found Moses and decided to raise him, but she needed help. She asked Jochebed to take care of Moses while he was little. Jochebed ended up being able to care for her son!

PHARAOH'S DAUGHTER

Exodus 2

HERO

☆ Princess in Egypt
☆ Daughter of Pharaoh
☆ Saved baby Moses

PHARAOH'S daughter was a princess. She lived a life filled with advantages and luxuries, but the princess took pity on Moses as a baby and cared for him.

One day, Pharaoh's daughter went to the Nile River. The princess saw a basket in the reeds and asked her maid to get it for her. The basket had a baby inside it!

WHAT SHOULD SHE DO?

Pharaoh's daughter knew her father had made a law declaring that Hebrew baby boys should be killed. But when she saw the baby crying, the princess felt sorry for him. "This is one of the Hebrew babies," she said. She decided to save him.

FAMILY HELP

The baby's sister, Miriam, was nearby and suggested she find a woman to help take care of the baby. Pharaoh's daughter agreed and made sure the baby was cared for until he was old enough to move into the palace. When the baby was older, the princess adopted him and named him Moses.

CHOOSING RIGHT OVER WRONG

The princess went against her own father's law and saved the Hebrew baby boy who touched her heart.

PHARAOH
OF THE EXODUS

Exodus 5–15

VILLAIN

☆ King of Egypt
☆ Ruled during time of Exodus

PHARAOH was a powerful king over all of Egypt. He had thousands of Israelite slaves. He was asked over and over again to set the slaves free, but despite the consequences, Pharaoh would not free them. He wanted to keep his slaves, so he could stay rich and mighty.

God wanted to free the Israelites. So he sent Moses and his brother, Aaron, to Pharaoh. God told them to tell Pharaoh to set the Israelites free.

HOLDING ON TO HIS SLAVES

Pharaoh answered, "Who is this LORD and why should I listen to him? I won't let the Israelites go." Pharaoh was annoyed that anyone would want him to give up his slaves. He became so angry that he ordered the Israelites to do more and harder work in the same amount of time.

THE PLAGUES

Moses and Aaron went back to Pharaoh time and time again. Each time, they said, "If you don't let the Israelites go, God will punish the Egyptians." Ten curses, called plagues, came over Egypt. Time and time

again, Pharaoh would get scared and agree to free the people.

But every time, Pharaoh changed his mind and kept the Israelites in slavery.

I CHANGED MY MIND

Finally, after Pharaoh's own son was killed in a plague, he agreed to let the Israelites go. But when the Israelites left, Pharaoh changed his mind again! He sent soldiers on chariots to bring back the slaves.

Carving of bound slaves near the entrance to the temple complex of Abu Simbel, Egypt

SWIMMING IN THE SEA

God divided the Red Sea in two and allowed the Israelites to walk through it. Once the slaves were on the other side and safe, God rushed the sea back together. Pharaoh and all his soldiers who were chasing the Israelites drowned in the crashing waves.

GAME OVER

Pharaoh didn't listen to God. His army, his land, his people, and even his own son were destroyed.

THE TEN PLAGUES

1. Water turned to blood.
2. Frogs invaded.
3. A giant cloud of gnats
4. Swarms of flies
5. All the Egyptian animals died.
6. Egyptians were covered in horrible boils.
7. Hailstorms
8. Swarms of locusts
9. Darkness
10. Firstborn sons died.

MOSES

Exodus, Numbers, Leviticus, Deuteronomy

HERO

★ Prince, shepherd, prophet, priest
★ Leader of the Israelites
★ Brother of Aaron and Miriam

MOSES was born at a difficult time for the Israelites. The Egyptians held the Israelites as slaves and treated them harshly. God chose Moses to help lead the people out of Egypt and into freedom. Throughout his life, Moses faced many scary challenges, but he trusted God to keep him and the people of Israel safe.

One day, Moses saw an Israelite slave being beaten by an Egyptian. Even though Moses could have been arrested or even killed for protecting a slave, he defended the slave and killed the Egyptian.

MIDIAN

To avoid being arrested, Moses ran away to the land of Midian to stay safe. In Midian, Moses became a shepherd.

THE BURNING BUSH

While on Mount Sinai one day, Moses saw a bush in flames. Even though the bush was on fire, it wasn't burning up. When Moses took a step toward this incredible sight, God called out to Moses, "I have heard the cry of my people, the Israelites. I am sending you to Pharaoh to lead my people out of Egypt."

I'M NOT SO SURE

Moses wanted his people to be free, but he was unsure of himself. Why would the Israelites follow him? Why would Pharaoh listen to him? God gave Moses signs and words to convince the people that God was with him. But Moses was still uncertain. God agreed to send Moses's brother, Aaron, to help him.

STANDING UP TO PHARAOH

Moses and Aaron went to Pharaoh (pp. 20–21). They had to stand up to the ruler of all of Egypt and tell him to free God's people. Moses warned Pharaoh that if he didn't free the Israelites, awful curses, called plagues, would make the Egyptians miserable. It took courage to threaten a ruler, but Moses wouldn't give up. He went back to Pharaoh over and over again. Finally, after ten plagues, Pharaoh agreed.

EXIT EGYPT

Moses led the Israelites out of slavery,
between the rushing walls of water of
the Red Sea, and out of Egypt.

THE EXODUS

The Bible says Moses led approximately
two million Israelites through the wilderness
toward the land God had promised them, the
land of Canaan, for forty years. The years
were long. Food and water were hard to find,
but God provided the Israelites with enough
food and water to survive.

NEVER GIVE UP

It was daring to confront Pharaoh and
scary and difficult to spend all those
years in the wilderness, leading millions
of people. But Moses stayed close to God
and never gave up.

AARON

Exodus 4, 7–8, 32; Numbers 18

GOD chose Aaron for a very special mission—to help his younger brother, Moses, free the Israelites from Egypt. Aaron willingly went with Moses to do the brave things God commanded. Aaron was influential in saving the Israelites and pointing them to God.

- ☆ First High Priest of Israel
- ☆ Son of Jochebed
- ☆ Brother of Moses and Isaac

Aaron was a talented speaker, and God made him Moses's spokesperson. God said, "When Pharaoh asks for a miracle, Aaron will throw down his staff and it will become a serpent. When Pharaoh won't listen, have Aaron hold out his staff to make the plagues come over Egypt."

MIRACLE WORKER

Even though Aaron had never done such amazing things before, Aaron trusted God and did as he commanded. When he threw his staff on the ground, it became a serpent. When he held his staff over the Nile River, the water turned to blood. When Aaron held his staff over the canals, frogs hopped out of the water and onto the land.

DID YOU KNOW?

Later, after the plagues, God made Aaron's staff flower with almond blossoms as a sign he was chosen to lead.

DID YOU KNOW?

While in the wilderness, the Israelites fought a battle against the army of Amalek. As long as Moses's arms were lifted in the air, the Israelites would win. But Moses's arms got tired. So Aaron and another man held Moses's arms up for him. The Israelites won the battle.

HIGH PRIEST

Aaron struggled to be faithful at times, but he loved and trusted God. God chose Aaron to be the first high priest of Israel.

RELYING ON GOD FOR COURAGE

God asked Aaron to do some scary but fantastic things—to confront powerful Pharaoh, to bring plagues to the land, to cross through the Red Sea, to travel the wilderness, and eventually to be priest over God's people. Aaron relied on God and faithfully obeyed him to accomplish these great things.

DID YOU KNOW?

Aaron is mentioned in Psalm 115:12: "The LORD remembers us and will bless us: He will bless his people Israel, he will bless the house of Aaron."

JETHRO

Exodus 2–4, 18

JETHRO was a kind, wise shepherd. He was also a judge who gave helpful advice to Moses.

When Moses helped Jethro's daughters at a well in Midian, Jethro was grateful and invited Moses to stay with him. Later, Jethro's daughter, Zipporah, married Moses and had two sons. Jethro kept Zipporah and Moses's sons safe in his home while Moses led the Israelites out of Egypt.

Jethro went to visit Moses in the wilderness to hear how God had rescued the Israelites. After hearing the story, Jethro yelled, "Praise God!"

Jethro saw that many of the Israelites came to Moses for advice. Jethro suggested that Moses put trustworthy men in charge to help the Israelites with their problems. Moses followed his father-in-law's recommendation and did just this. Jethro's advice allowed Moses to focus on his role in leading the people of Israel.

MIRIAM

Exodus 2, 15; Numbers 12

MIRIAM was a musician and prophet, who helped rescue her brother Moses when she was young. Later she worked with Moses and Aaron to save the Israelites.

When Miriam was a girl, her mother had her watch her brother Moses, whom they had hidden from Pharaoh. When Pharaoh's daughter found the baby in the river, clever Miriam asked the princess if she wanted to have Moses's mother help care for him. In this way, Miriam helped her mother care for her own child.

Later, Miriam traveled with her brothers, Aaron and Moses, as they led the Israelites out of Egypt. After Pharaoh and his men died in the rushing Red Sea, Miriam grabbed a tambourine and led others in a song. "Sing to the LORD, for he has triumphed gloriously."

JOSHUA

Joshua 1–6

HERO

☆ Warrior
☆ Led Israelite army against Jericho

WHEN Moses died, God told Joshua it was time for him to lead the Israelites. God assured Joshua that he would always be with him. The Israelites respected Joshua and trusted him as their new leader.

God promised to give the Israelites the land of Canaan, but they would need to conquer the people who lived there and capture the city of Jericho. How would the Israelite army capture this city that was surrounded by a giant stone wall?

A CRAZY PLAN

God had a plan. He said, "Have the soldiers march once around the city for six days." The priests were to lead this parade around Jericho, carrying the ark of the covenant. On the seventh day, they were to march around the city seven times, with the priests blowing trumpets. On the seventh circle around the city that day, as the trumpets blew one long blast, all the people should shout—and the walls would crumble. This plan sounded crazy. How could soldiers overtake a city by marching in circles and shouting?

DID THE PLAN WORK?

Joshua did exactly as God said. On the seventh day, when the Israelites circled the city the seventh time, they shouted—and the walls of Jericho crashed to the ground. Joshua and his army defeated Jericho!

KORAH

Numbers 16

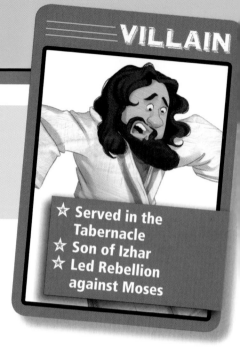

KORAH had a special job. But Korah craved more power and riches. Instead of gaining more, Korah ended up losing everything.

☆ Served in the Tabernacle
☆ Son of Izhar
☆ Led Rebellion against Moses

Korah served in the tent where the Israelites worshiped God, called the tabernacle. This was an important job, but it wasn't enough for Korah. He wanted to be in charge, like Moses and Aaron. Korah convinced more than 250 men to oppose Aaron and Moses as their leaders. Korah said, "Why do you think you get to be in charge?"

SPECIAL WORK FOR EVERYONE

Moses knew God had given different people different work. Moses told Korah, "God has given you so much. He has given you special work. Why are you challenging God's instructions?" Korah wouldn't listen. Instead he stirred up even more people and created an uprising.

A HOLE IN THE GROUND

God was furious because Korah was turning the Israelites against the leaders God had chosen. God told Moses to warn the people to step back. Then God opened a giant hole in the ground. Korah, his family, his supporters, his tents, and all his things were sucked down into the hole and disappeared forever!

UNSATISFIED

Korah wasn't satisfied with the role he'd been given. Because he opposed God and turned others away from him, Korah and his plans were destroyed.

RAHAB

Joshua 2, 6

HERO

RAHAB lived in the town of Jericho—the town God had promised the Israelites. Rahab realized the Lord was the supreme God. She risked her life to protect people she didn't know, because they were sent from God.

☆ Lived in Jericho
☆ Mother of Boaz
☆ Helped the Israelites

Two of Joshua's spies snuck into Jericho to look around. They stopped at Rahab's house.

The king sent men to ask Rahab if she knew anything about the spies. Rahab knew she should obey the king. She knew she could be punished for hiding spies. But Rahab protected the Israelites. Rahab bravely told the king's men, "Those spies were here. But they already left town, and I don't know where they went."

WHAT WAS SHE HIDING?

Rahab did know where the men were! She'd hidden them on her roof, under some straw. Later, Rahab helped the spies sneak out her window.

WHY THE RED ROPE?

Before the men left, Rahab begged them to keep her and her family safe when the Israelites returned to conquer the city. The spies told Rahab to hang a red rope from her window so they would know whom to save.

PROMISE KEEPERS

When the Israelite army destroyed Jericho, the men came back and rescued Rahab and her family. Rahab had courageously protected the Israelite men to honor God, and now those men protected her.

ACHAN

Joshua 7

ACHAN was more concerned about being rich than about following God's directions. And in the end, Achan's greed ruined him.

God told the Israelites to destroy everything in Jericho—except some specific treasures that were supposed to be put aside for God.

Achan heard God's orders from his commander, Joshua, but Achan didn't listen. Instead of giving the treasure to God, Achan stole a beautiful robe, two hundred silver coins, and a bar of gold. He hid the riches under his tent and buried the silver and acted like he hadn't done anything wrong.

GOD KNEW WHO DID IT

But God knew what Achan had done. As punishment for Achan's crime, the Israelites lost their next battle. God told Joshua, "One of your people has stolen the valuables I told you to set aside for me. I'll show you who did it."

CAUGHT

Joshua gathered the people, and God pointed to Achan. Achan admitted his crime. He and his family were punished for disobeying God, stealing, lying, and trying to hide Achan's greed.

Because Achan thought having treasure was more important than following God's instructions, he and many others were punished.

DID YOU KNOW?

The valuables God wanted set aside for him were bronze, silver, gold, and iron.

DEBORAH

Judges 4–5

HERO

★ Prophet
★ First and only female judge
★ Songwriter

DEBORAH was the first and only female judge in Israel. She gave people advice and helped to settle the Israelites' disagreements fairly and wisely.

Deborah would sit under a palm tree named Deborah's Palm and help the Israelites solve their arguments. God spoke to Deborah and gave her messages for the people.

ATTACK SISERA

One day, God told Deborah that a man named Barak should take ten thousand warriors and attack the army of a man named Sisera. Barak was frightened. He told Deborah he would only go if she went with him. Deborah agreed to help but warned Barak that he wouldn't get credit for the victory.

CONFIDENT IN BATTLE

Deborah was confident God would win the battle. She marched with Barak and his ten thousand soldiers to the river. She told Barak, "The Lord is marching before you. God will win this battle."

DEBORAH'S SONG

The Israelites killed every single one of Sisera's warriors that day. Deborah and Barak sang a song about the battle and gave praise for their victory to God.

DID YOU KNOW?
People sing praises to God throughout the Bible. The Israelites sang praises to God when they made it across the Red Sea. King David often sang praises to God.

31

GIDEON

Judges 6–8

GIDEON was considered a weak member of one of the least important families. He was frightened when God found him. Although Gideon didn't feel like a hero, God turned him into one.

HERO

★ Farmer
★ Led Israelites in battle against Midianites
★ Judge

One day, Gideon was hiding because he was afraid of the Midianites, who were cruel to the Israelites. An angel said, "Mighty hero, the Lord is with you! I am sending you to rescue Israel." Gideon didn't feel mighty at all. But God said, "I will be with you."

WOOL FLEECE

Gideon was still uncertain. He asked God for a sign. "Make the wool fleece I lay down wet and the ground dry." God made the fleece wet and the ground dry. Gideon still wasn't convinced. He asked God to do the same thing—except backward—the next night. God made the ground wet and the fleece dry.

HOW BIG WAS HIS ARMY?

It was time to fight, and Gideon took thirty-two thousand men with him to fight the Midianites. God shrunk Gideon's army to only three hundred men. Gideon again felt small and incapable, but he trusted God.

HORNS, POTS, AND TORCHES

Gideon gathered his men around a camp of thousands of Midianites. Gideon told his army, "Take a horn, a pot, and a torch. Blow your horns, yell, and smash your pots so your torches shine." Gideon's army did as he said. All the noise and bright lights frightened the enemy. They ran around mixed-up, trying to escape, and God made the Midianites confused so they would kill each other.

MIGHTY WARRIOR

Gideon didn't feel strong or powerful, but God transformed him into a mighty warrior. And Gideon's small army, without weapons, was victorious.

SAMSON

Judges 13–16

HERO

☆ Judge
☆ Nazirite
☆ Possessed great strength

SAMSON was a daring, long-haired judge of the Israelites. His life was dedicated to God. Throughout his years, Samson used his super strength to save the Israelites from the Philistines.

Before Samson was born, an angel told his mother she would have a son who would help rescue Israel from Philistine. As a sign of his commitment to God, the boy should never cut his hair. Samson's parents followed the angel's instructions.

SUPER STRONG

God gave Samson super strength. Samson tapped into this strength to rip a lion's jaw apart with his hands, to break free of ropes, to kill one thousand Philistines using only the jawbone of a donkey, and to carry the town gates to the top of a hill.

CAPTURED

Samson judged Israel for twenty years, but he was eventually captured by his enemies, the Philistines. They beat Samson and put him in jail.

FINAL ACT OF STRENGTH

At a festival, the Philistines stood Samson between two pillars of their temple to make fun of him. Samson asked God for strength one last time. Samson pushed the pillars down, and the temple crashed onto Samson and killed three thousand Philistines. Repeatedly Samson used the amazing strength God gave him to rescue his people and destroy their enemies.

DELILAH

Judges 16

DELILAH isn't famous for her strength, intelligence, sense of humor, or beauty. In fact, we know very little about her. But we do know that the strong judge of Israel, Samson, was in love with her. And instead of loving him back, Delilah agreed to trick him for money.

☆ Betrayed Samson
☆ Lived in the Sorek Valley

The leaders of Samson's enemies, the Philistine rulers, told Delilah they would each give her 1,100 pieces of silver if she could find out what would make super-strong Samson weak.

SAMSON'S SECRET

She asked Samson, "Where do you get your incredible strength?"

Samson said, "If I'm tied up with seven new bow strings, I can't break free."

So while Samson was sleeping, Delilah tied him up with strings. She was tricky and hid the Philistine men in her house, ready to kill Samson. But the strings couldn't hold Samson. He broke free and escaped.

Two more times, Delilah begged Samson to tell her his secret. Two more times, Delilah tied Samson up while he was sleeping and had men waiting to attack. But both times, Samson escaped.

A HAIRCUT

Delilah didn't give up on her evil plan. She pleaded with Samson to tell her what would make him weak. Finally, Samson told Delilah, "If you cut my hair, I will lose my superhuman strength." While Samson was sleeping, Delilah had a man cut his hair, and the Philistines attacked him and put him in jail.

WHAT DID IT COST?

Delilah was stubborn. She did not abandon her sneaky plan until she succeeded. She got her silver, but she lost Samson's trust and companionship.

RUTH

Ruth 1–4

HERO

RUTH was loyal and brave. When her husband and father-in-law died, life seemed hopeless for Ruth and her mother-in-law, Naomi. Ruth could either stay in her homeland of Moab and move back with her parents, or leave and go with Naomi to Bethlehem.

☆ Wife, mother, friend
☆ Wife of Naomi's son
☆ Later married Boaz
☆ Mother of Obed

Even though it meant leaving her family, her country, and her home, Ruth loved her mother-in-law and chose to go with her to Bethlehem. Ruth and Naomi didn't have land, jobs, or food. But poor people could gather grain from the edges of farmers' fields. Ruth had promised to care for Naomi, so she went to the fields and gathered food.

BOAZ

The owner of the field Ruth was picking grain from was a kind man named Boaz. When Ruth and Naomi realized Boaz was one of Naomi's distant relatives, Ruth took another risk—she asked Boaz to care for her and Naomi! Ruth knew if Boaz agreed to care for them, she and Naomi could have a home, food, and safety.

A NEW LIFE

Boaz and Ruth married and had a son. They took Naomi into their home. Because of Ruth's bravery and love for Naomi, they were able to live a happy new life.

DID YOU KNOW?
A law said that said farmers had to leave the edges of their field unharvested for poor people to gather food. This was called *gleaning*.

SAMUEL

1 Samuel 1–4, 7–13, 15–16, 25

SAMUEL spent his life listening to and pointing people to God. When he was a boy, his family sent him to live with the high priest Eli, so Samuel could learn how to serve God. Samuel grew up to be a great prophet, priest, and judge for Israel. God gave Samuel messages, and Samuel could hear God speak!

☆ Judge, Priest, Prophet
☆ Last Judge of Israel
☆ Anointer of Kings

When Samuel was old, the Israelites asked for a king. Samuel warned them that they didn't need a human king—they already had God as their perfect king. But the Israelites wanted a human king.

ANOINTING THE FIRST KING

God allowed the people to have their king, and Samuel followed God's instructions. He anointed the man God chose as king, Saul. When Saul became king, Samuel reminded the Israelites to worship and listen to God.

WISE COUNCIL FOR THE KING

Samuel shared God's plans with Saul. He also worked hard to make Saul understand how important it was to listen to God.

ANOINTING ANOTHER KING

Later, God told Samuel to anoint David to be the new king of Israel. Samuel once again followed God's directions. Samuel spent his life doing what God asked of him and pointing people to the one true God.

Urn of oil for anointing

DID YOU KNOW?

Samuel's mother begged God for a son. She promised she would give her boy to God. God answered Hannah's prayer by giving her Samuel. Hannah kept her promise and took Samuel to learn from the high priest Eli when he was still a toddler.

36

SAUL

1 Samuel 9–24, 26, 28, 31

SAUL was strong, tall, and handsome. He was chosen by God, so it seemed likely he would be the perfect first king of Israel. But Saul kept trying to do things his own way.

Saul was not a good listener. When God told Saul to wait for Samuel to give an offering, Saul didn't wait. When God told Saul to attack and destroy the Amalekites and all their possessions, Saul attacked but didn't destroy everything. He and his people saved the most valuable animals, even though God had told him not to.

When Samuel asked Saul about it, Saul lied and said, "I did obey God."

JEALOUS

Saul became extremely jealous of David. He spent years trying to kill David, even though David was one of Saul's best warriors. Saul was so jealous that he almost killed his own son, Jonathan, because of Jonathan's friendship with David.

THE REIGN IS OVER

Because Saul wouldn't obey God, God decided to make someone else king. Saul eventually died in a bloody battle, surrounded by the Philistines.

SECONDARY STORY: FROM GOOD TO BAD

Saul had everything the Hebrew people thought a king should have—he came from a wealthy family, was good-looking, and had a mighty appearance. But just because someone looks like a "hero" doesn't mean that they are one. Saul had the potential to be a great king, but his selfishness ruined him.

Q: Have you ever tried to do something your own way even though a parent, teacher, or coach told you to do it differently? How did it turn out?

DAVID

1 Samuel 16–31; 2 Samuel

HERO

☆ Shepherd, musician, soldier, king
☆ Second king of Israel
☆ Forefather of Jesus
☆ Writer of Psalms

DAVID wanted to please God in everything he did. And God saw how much David loved him and chose David to be king. To this day, David is considered by many to be the greatest king of Israel.

David was a shepherd and the youngest of all of Jesse's sons. No one, not even his father or brothers, thought he would be chosen as king. But when King Saul disobeyed God, God chose David as the next king of Israel. God was with David.

PATIENT HONOR

David honored the fact that Saul was still king for many years. David was a gifted musician and played songs to calm King Saul. David became one of the greatest soldiers in Saul's army, winning numerous battles. He defeated the enormous champion of the enemy's army, Goliath—with only a slingshot! Even though David helped Saul, Saul was jealous of David and planned to kill him. David had many chances to kill Saul, but he didn't.

KING AT LAST

David trusted God and God's timing. After Saul was killed in battle, David finally took over as king of Israel. He was thirty years old at the time.

CONVERSATIONS WITH GOD

Throughout his entire life, David talked to God. He asked God for advice. He thanked God when things went well. David cried out to God when he was hurt or angry and when he was ashamed of his mistakes. David wrote songs to praise God.

Q: David talked to God about everything. How often do you talk to God?

PSALM 23,
A SONG OF DAVID

The LORD is my shepherd, I lack nothing.
He makes me lie down in green pastures,
He leads me beside quiet waters,
He refreshes my soul.
He guides me along the right paths for his name's sake.
Even though I walk through the darkest valley
I will fear no evil, for you are with me;
Your rod and your staff, they comfort me.
You prepare a table before me in the presence
    of my enemies.
You anoint my head with oil; my cup
    overflows.
Surely your goodness and love will
    follow me
All the days of my life,
And I will dwell in the house
    of the LORD forever.

GOLIATH

1 Samuel 17

VILLAIN

☆ Philistine Champion
☆ More than nine feet tall
☆ Battled young David

GOLIATH was the Philistine champion. He towered over all the other men! He threatened people, cursed the God of Israel, and worshiped other gods. Goliath was taken down by an opponent who relied on the Lord.

Goliath challenged the army of Israel to send their best man to fight against him. He did this for forty days. But no Israelite was brave enough to fight him. They were scared. He was so much bigger than they were, and he had the best armor and weapons. Then a shepherd boy named David said, "I'll fight him."

WHAT'S THAT? A ROCK?

Goliath laughed when he saw young David with only a slingshot. Goliath called David nasty names. But it didn't bother David. David trusted God and God's strength to win the fight. David pulled out a sling and hurled a stone at Goliath. The rock hit the giant between the eyes and knocked him down. Goliath fell flat on his face. David walked over, took Goliath's sword, and killed him once and for all.

THE END OF A BULLY

Goliath was convinced that he could beat anybody and everybody all by himself. He scared people by bullying them. In the end, all Goliath's strength and might couldn't compete against a shepherd boy who trusted God to win the battle.

Q: Is there a bully at your school or in your neighborhood? How would it feel to stand up to that person?

JONATHAN

1 Samuel 13–14, 19–20, 31; 2 Samuel 1

HERO

★ Soldier, Friend
★ Son of King Saul
★ Brother of Michal

JONATHAN was a brave warrior who fought for his father, King Saul, in Israel's army. He was also a loyal friend to David.

Jonathan trusted in God for victory. During a battle, when the rest of the army panicked, Jonathan stayed calm. He and his armor bearer surprise-attacked twenty Philistines, which scared the rest of their army into running away. The battle was won because of Jonathan's bravery.

BEST FRIENDS

Jonathan became best friends with David. They loved each other like brothers. When Saul became jealous of David, Jonathan defended his best friend, but he continued to fight for Saul's army because it was his duty. Jonathan also stayed true to David. Even though he knew Saul could punish him for protecting David, Jonathan continued to warn David about Saul's attacks.

DID YOU KNOW?

During one very long, tiring battle, King Saul gave an order for his troops not to eat anything. Jonathan didn't hear the order. When he found some honey in the forest, Jonathan ate it. The honey gave Jonathan energy and strength.

BRAVE TILL THE END

Jonathan died in a battle defending his people from their enemy, the Philistines. He lived his life bravely, loving his best friend and always doing what he thought was right.

Q: Who is your best friend? How do you help each other?

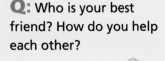

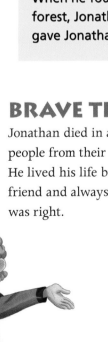

MICHAL

1 Samuel 19

MICHAL loved and married David, one of her father, King Saul's, warriors. But Michal soon had to choose between her father and her husband.

Michal overheard King Saul telling his troops to attack David. She knew her father could punish her for helping David, but she loved him. So Michal lowered David out the window, where no one would see him.

Michal put a statue under the covers of the bed, with goat hair at the top, so it would look like David was still in bed. She told the soldiers who came looking for him that David was sick. The soldiers were fooled, and David escaped. Michal risked her life and reputation to save her husband from her father.

ABIGAIL

1 Samuel 25

BEAUTIFUL Abigail used her intelligence to serve the Lord. She decided to choose what was right, even when it went against what her unwise husband, Nabal, did.

When David was in the wilderness, he sent his troops to ask Abigail's husband, Nabal, for food from Nabal's feast. Nabal said no. Abigail thought Nabal was being foolish for not helping the future king. She feared that if they didn't help David, his troops would attack. So Abigail took all kinds of food to David and apologized for her husband's actions. David blessed Abigail and promised not to attack her people.

Abigail's wise decision saved them.

Abigail was honest, so the next day she told Nabal what she'd done. Nabal was so shocked, his heart stopped. He died ten days later.

Since Abigail no longer had a husband and David appreciated her kindness, honesty, and wisdom, he married Abigail. Abigail served her husband, King David, for the rest of her life.

MEDIUM OF EN-DOR

1 Samuel 28

☆ Fortuneteller
☆ Lived in En-dor

THERE was a medium—a sorcerer who claimed to have magic powers—who lived in En-dor. God had told the Israelites to stay away from sorcery of any kind, but she continued to practice her sorcery.

King Saul made it illegal to practice sorcery and made all the mediums move out of his land, but this woman kept doing sorcery. One day Saul asked God for advice and God didn't answer. Saul was scared and desperate, and he went to visit the medium. He wore a disguise so no one would recognize him visiting the illegal medium.

SAVING HERSELF

The medium was clever. She didn't want to get arrested, so the first thing she said was, "The king has made it against the law to be a medium. If I help you, I could be killed." Saul promised he would protect the medium and begged her to call the prophet Samuel from the dead.

EEEEK!

The medium called Samuel and screamed when she saw him. She said to Saul, "Why have you tricked me? You are Saul!" But Saul told her not be afraid.

WHAT DID SAMUEL SAY?

Saul begged Samuel for advice, but he refused to help Saul. Samuel reminded Saul that he had turned away from God. Now God had turned away from Saul. Samuel also warned Saul that he and his sons would die the next day in battle.

THAT WAS SCARY!

The medium of En-dor intentionally broke the law. Even though she was breaking the law, she comforted Saul after Samuel told him he and his sons would die.

NATHAN

2 Samuel 7, 12

☆ Prophet
☆ Advisor to King David
☆ Name means "God has given"

NATHAN was a prophet who boldly spoke the messages given by God, even when they were difficult to share. When David became king of Israel, God sent Nathan to help David understand God's will.

Nathan shared many messages from God with David. When David wanted to give the ark of the covenant a beautiful home, Nathan explained that God didn't want him to build a house for the ark. He said God's plan was for David's son to build such a place. Nathan also told David that God would always bless David and his family would continue as kings over Israel.

CORRECTING THE KING

When David took his soldier Uriah's wife, Nathan reminded David that God had given him everything—the throne, riches, power. Nathan helped David realize how selfish he'd been. Nathan told David that God forgave him, but there would be consequences.

LOYALTY

Nathan stayed loyal to King David even when some of the Israelites left David's side. Throughout his life, Nathan was faithful to God and God's messages, even when they were challenging to deliver.

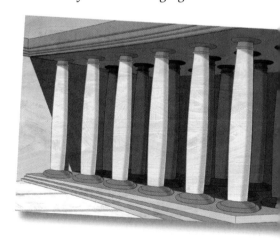

DID YOU KNOW?

Samuel was the prophet God sent to advise King Saul, and Nathan was the prophet God sent to advise King David.

44

ABSALOM

2 Samuel 13–19

===== VILLAIN
☆ Son of King David
☆ Brother of Tamar
☆ Half-brother of Amnon, Kileab, and Solomon

ABSALOM was conceited and violent. His desire for power destroyed him. When he was furious with his half-brother Amnon, Absalom had him killed.

Absalom entered the city each morning, trying to charm the visitors coming to see King David into thinking he was more wonderful and important than his father. As part of his plan to take over as king, Absalom spent years convincing the crowds to like him.

Eventually, David and Absalom's armies battled to see who would be king.

Absalom tried to escape in the forest, but his long hair got caught in a tree. He was killed by one of David's men.

Absalom tried to do everything with force. He murdered his brother, battled for the throne, and was killed. Even in death, Absalom's actions caused pain. His father, David, was filled with sorrow when his son died.

ADONIJAH

1 Kings 1–2

===== VILLAIN
☆ Son of King David
☆ Brother of Absalom, Amnon, Solomon, and Daniel

WHEN David was old, his son Adonijah decided he wanted to be king. He plotted how to take the throne from his father. When one plan didn't work, Adonijah would try another one.

Adonijah made a sacrifice to God, thinking this would make him king. He even threw a party to celebrate. When Nathan (p. 44) discovered the plan, he told David. David had Solomon, who was chosen to be the next king, anointed immediately. When Adonijah heard, he threw his arms around the altar to keep from being dragged away for what he'd done.

Adonijah begged the new king to forgive him. Solomon forgave his brother under the condition that Adonijah wouldn't cause any more trouble.

But Adonijah still wanted the throne. When Solomon heard another scheme of Adonijah's to gain power, Solomon had him killed. Adonijah's quest for power ruined him.

SOLOMON

2 Samuel 12; 1 Kings 1–11; 2 Chronicles 8

HERO

★ King
★ Builder
★ Son of King David and Bathsheba
★ Brothers: Absalom, Adonijah

KING Solomon is considered in the Bible to be one of the wisest men who ever lived. He longed for wisdom to rule his people well.

When King David was old, his son Solomon was anointed as the new king. Solomon loved God, and God loved and blessed Solomon. One day, God told Solomon, "I'll give you anything you want. What would you like?"

A WISE HEART

Solomon told God, "What I want most is wisdom to know the difference between right and wrong, so I can be a good king for you, LORD." Solomon could have asked for power, riches, or fame, but he asked for wisdom. God said, "I will give you what you asked for—a wise heart. And I will also bless you with riches and a long life."

THE TEMPLE

One of Solomon's greatest accomplishments was building the first temple for God. It was magnificent! The temple was ninety feet long, thirty feet wide, and forty-five feet high. It was built out of cedar and cypress wood and covered in gold. The doors and posts were carved with decorations of flowers, trees, and angels. It took thousands of men seven years to build this temple for God.

DID YOU KNOW?
Solomon is said to have written some of the Bible, including Ecclesiastes and Song of Songs. The Bible also says that Solomon wrote 3,000 proverbs and 1,005 songs.

A THRIVING KINGDOM

Solomon's kingdom was great.
He ruled far and wide. He
knew how to rule his people,
but Solomon also knew about
plants, animals, birds, and fish.
Solomon's kingdom flourished.
While Solomon was king of Israel,
all of Israel lived peacefully.

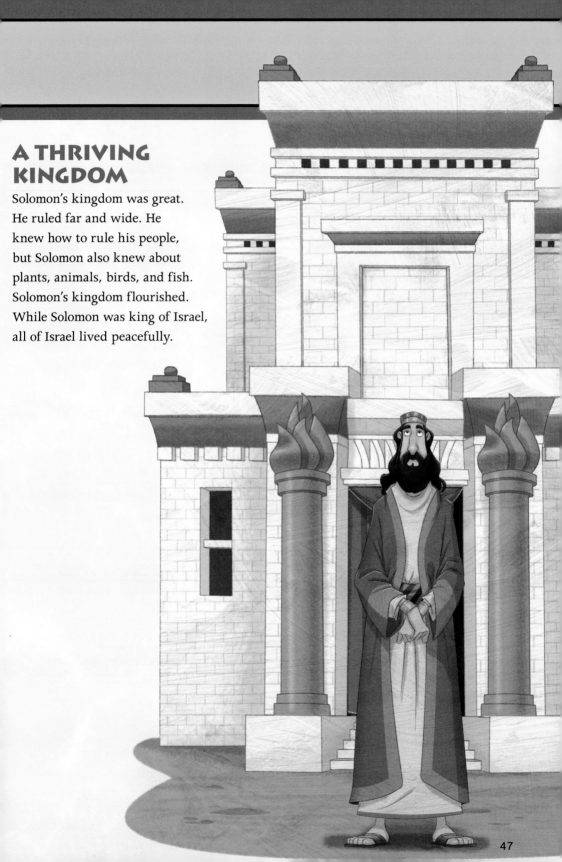

JEROBOAM

1 Kings 11–14

☆ King of northern kingdom of Israel
☆ Reigned from 931–910 BC
☆ Son of Nebat
☆ Father of Abijah and Nadab

JEROBOAM was chosen by God to take over ten of the twelve tribes of Israel from Solomon. But Jeroboam turned away from God and lost everything.

God told Jeroboam, "If you listen to me and follow my ways, I will always be with you. I will create a great kingdom for you."

Jeroboam loved the idea of being king, but he didn't fully trust God. So Jeroboam set up his throne in Ephraim. He was afraid if his people went back to Jerusalem to worship God at the temple, they would leave him and follow Solomon.

TWO GOLDEN CALVES

Then Jeroboam did something horrible. He made golden calves and put them in Ephraim. He told the people that they were the god that had brought the Israelites out of Egypt.

NOT LISTENING

God was furious. He sent a prophet to warn Jeroboam. But Jeroboam wouldn't listen. God sent Jeroboam another message: "Because you haven't listened to me, your family will be destroyed. I will raise a new king who will overtake your kingdom."

A WASTED CHANCE

Jeroboam had the chance to be a great king and to rule over ten tribes of Israel. But he turned away from God and lost everything.

48

ELIJAH

1 Kings 17–19; 2 Kings 1–2

HERO

★ Prophet and miracle worker
★ Lived during the reign of King Ahab
★ Challenged prophets of Baal

ELIJAH was a great prophet. Even in the toughest situations, Elijah trusted God. And God always cared for Elijah.

God told Elijah to warn King Ahab that a drought was coming. There would be years with no rain. It was dangerous to tell the king bad news, but Elijah obeyed.

God knew Ahab blamed Elijah for the drought, so God told Elijah to hide. God had ravens bring Elijah food and provided fresh water from a brook every day.

MY GOD IS BETTER THAN YOUR GOD

Years later, Elijah was the only prophet left who worshiped God. Elijah loved God and wanted to show the Israelites that God was real. Elijah told the people to make an altar for their god, Baal. Elijah made an altar for God. Elijah said, "Whoever sets fire to the wood on the altar is the true God." Nothing happened at Baal's altar. God's altar burst into flames. God even burned the stones and dust. All the people cried, "The LORD is God!"

GOD PROVIDES

Elijah continued to love and obey God his entire life, and God kept him safe. When Elijah was weak, God fed him. When Elijah was exhausted, God strengthened him. When people tried to kill Elijah, God protected him.

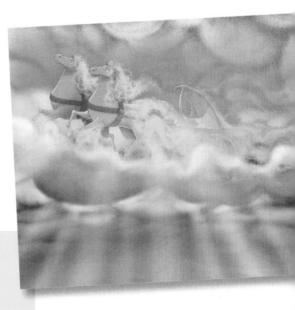

DID YOU KNOW?

Did you know? Elijah was taken to heaven in a chariot of fire.

ELISHA

1 Kings 19; 2 Kings 2–9, 13

WHEN the prophet Elijah went to heaven, he left his cloak as a sign that Elisha would take his place. Elisha was God's prophet for sixty-five years. During that time, God performed incredible miracles through Elisha.

Elisha hit the Jordan River with Elijah's cloak. The river divided in two, and Elisha walked across on dry land. When the water in Jericho was polluted and made people sick, Elisha sprinkled salt in the water and with God's help made it clean and clear to drink.

MORE WATER

When King Jehoshaphat and his army were in the wilderness without water, Elisha told the king that God would provide water. The next morning, the valleys overflowed with water.

MIRACLES FOR GOD

When God told him to, Elisha made blind men see and men with sight blind. Elisha turned poisonous food into healthy food. Elisha multiplied a little bit of grain and bread into enough food for a hundred people. With God's power, Elisha even raised a dead boy to life!

Elisha spent his life doing marvelous things for God's glory.

Q: Which one of Elisha's miracles is the most amazing to you?

JEZEBEL

1 Kings 16, 18–19, 21; 2 Kings 9

VILLAIN

☆ Queen
☆ Wife of Ahab, king of Israel
☆ Troublemaker

QUEEN Jezebel was married to evil King Ahab. She was sneaky and evil. Jezebel used her royal power to influence her husband and the people to turn away from God.

Jezebel had all the prophets of God killed. Only Elijah (p. 49) escaped.

IN THE NAME OF AHAB

One day, King Ahab was angry that a man wouldn't sell his vineyard to him. Jezebel said, "I'll get it for you."

Jezebel wrote letters telling the people to blame the vineyard owner, Naboth, for saying bad things about God and the king. Jezebel's letters also instructed the men to kill Naboth as punishment for bad things he didn't even say! Jezebel was deceptive. She signed the letters with Ahab's name so it looked like they were from the king. The people had to obey the king's commands, so they blamed and killed Naboth.

"Naboth is dead. Now you can have his vineyard," Jezebel told Ahab.

UNHAPPY ENDING

Eventually Jezebel was exposed for her wickedness and thrown out a window, where she fell to her death. Jezebel lived a selfish life. She lied, cheated, and killed to get her own way.

DID YOU KNOW?

Forgery is signing someone else's name to an important paper. It is illegal to commit forgery in the United States. Jezebel forged King Ahab's name on the letters she sent.

ATHALIAH

2 Kings 11

VILLAIN

☆ Queen
☆ Wife of King Jeroham
☆ Daughter of King Ahab

ATHALIAH was the daughter of a king and married a king. But Athaliah was evil. She wanted to destroy the royal family and take the throne for herself.

Athaliah married a mean ruler, Jehoram, king of Judah. When Jehoram died, Ahaziah, their son, became king. Ahaziah died after reigning only one year. Ahaziah's oldest son should have taken the throne next, but Athaliah wanted to be the ruler! Athaliah killed Ahaziah's sons—her own grandchildren!—so they couldn't rule. She stepped in as ruler of Judah.

HIDE-AND-GO-SEEK

Athaliah didn't know it, but her youngest grandson, Joash, was hidden. After Athaliah had ruled as queen for six years, the high priest announced that the rightful king was alive. The people found Joash in the temple and cried out, "Long live the king!" The guards grabbed Athaliah and took her to the palace, where she was killed.

CAN I SIT HERE?

Although Athaliah lived her life close to the throne, she wanted to be the one sitting on it. She did one of the cruelest things possible—she killed her own family to steal the position of ruler. But the true heir to the throne was eventually given his place as king.

HEZEKIAH

2 Kings 18–20; 2 Chronicles 29–33; Isaiah 36–39

HERO

★ King of Judah
★ Ruled from about 716–687 BC

HEZEKIAH was one of the most adored kings of Israel. For years, many kings of Israel had also worshiped idols. Hezekiah got rid of many of these idols and brought the Israelites back to God.

Hezekiah had all the idols destroyed and the altars where people worshiped other gods torn down. The beautiful temple King Solomon built for God had been locked up, but Hezekiah opened the doors so people could worship God again.

WILL YOU HEAL ME?

Hezekiah trusted God and prayed to him often. When Hezekiah was sick and thought he was going to die, he begged God to heal him. God rewarded Hezekiah's faithfulness and healed Hezekiah, letting him live fifteen more years.

BACK TO GOD

Hezekiah spent his life and his time as king bringing his people back to the God of Israel, the God who loved them.

DID YOU KNOW?

In the 1800s, archaeologists found a tunnel that was most likely built by Hezekiah. You can walk through it even today!

SENNACHERIB

2 Kings 18–19; 2 Chronicles 32; Isaiah 37

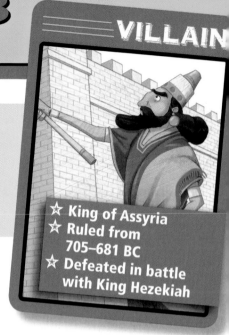

VILLAIN

SENNACHERIB was a powerful king from Assyria. Judah promised to pay him for protection but broke their promise. Sennacherib was angry. He wanted his money and revenge.

☆ King of Assyria
☆ Ruled from 705–681 BC
☆ Defeated in battle with King Hezekiah

Sennacherib brought a huge army and conquered all the land except Jerusalem.

Sennacherib told King Hezekiah he'd have to pay 22,500 pounds of silver if he wanted to save Jerusalem from attack. Hezekiah gave Sennacherib all the silver in the temple and the treasure from the palace.

DON'T TRUST HIM

Sennacherib sent a messenger telling the people of Jerusalem not to trust King Hezekiah and not to believe that the Lord would rescue them.

YOU'RE SURROUNDED

Sennacherib's army blocked the roads to Jerusalem so no one could escape and no food could get in. But King Hezekiah stored up food for his people and dug a tunnel to bring water into the city. Sennacherib's army waited, but Hezekiah and his people would not give up.

AND THE WINNER IS...

According to the Bible, God sent an angel, who killed 185,000 of the Assyrians. Sennacherib and his army ran away.

DID YOU KNOW?

When archaeologists discovered Sennacherib's palace in the 1800s, they found a cylinder with a history of battles carved into it.

MANASSEH

2 Chronicles 33

☆ King of Judah
☆ Son of Hezekiah
☆ Ruled from 697–643 BC
☆ Later forgiven by God

MANASSEH became king when he was only twelve years old. His father, Hezekiah, was a wonderful king, but Manasseh was awful. After realizing how terrible he'd been, Manasseh told God he was sorry. God forgave Manasseh for his evil.

Manasseh rebuilt the altars and temples to other gods that his father had torn down. Manasseh even built altars to other gods in God's temple, the one Solomon had built.

EVEN WORSE

Manasseh did many more horrible things. He turned his kingdom into an evil nation. God told Manasseh to change, but King Manasseh and all of Judah ignored God.

CAPTURED

To get Manasseh's attention, God sent the king of Assyria to capture him. Manasseh was chained and put on a leash that attached with a hook in his nose! He was taken far away, to Babylon.

I'M SORRY!

Manasseh felt horrible about his wicked deeds and begged God for forgiveness.

SECOND CHANCE

Even though Manasseh had been villainous, God forgave him. Manasseh was set free and sent home. When Manasseh returned to Jerusalem, he tore down the altars and temples to false gods. Manasseh made peace offerings to the Lord and told the people to worship only the one true God.

Q: How old are you? Would you be ready to be king or queen on your twelfth birthday?

55

JONAH

Jonah

GOD gave Jonah direct messages for the people. Jonah learned that when God calls you to do something, you should do it. Jonah also learned God forgives mistakes.

God told Jonah to go to Nineveh and tell the Ninevites that God would forgive them if they changed their wicked ways. Jonah feared the horrible Ninevites. He didn't want to go to their land. So, he got on a boat going the opposite direction.

MAN OVERBOARD

God reminded Jonah that he was supposed to be going to Nineveh by causing a storm that tossed the boat. Even though he was afraid, Jonah asked the crew to throw him overboard. When they did, the storm stopped.

IN THE BELLY OF A FISH

God sent a giant fish to swallow Jonah. Can you imagine how big it must have been? Jonah prayed to God and asked God to save him. Jonah said, "I cried out to the LORD in my great trouble, and he answered me." God heard Jonah's prayers and had the fish spit him out on dry, safe land.

Q: What's the biggest fish you've ever seen? Can you imagine being inside its belly for three days?

MESSAGE SENT

Jonah went to Nineveh and delivered God's message. When the Ninevites heard it, they stopped their evil ways and turned to God.

OKAY, GOD

Even though it was scary, Jonah ended up following God's instructions. When he did, God protected Jonah and Nineveh was saved.

DID YOU KNOW?

Jesus told his disciples that just like Jonah was inside a fish for three days, he would be in the tomb for three days.

ISAIAH

Isaiah

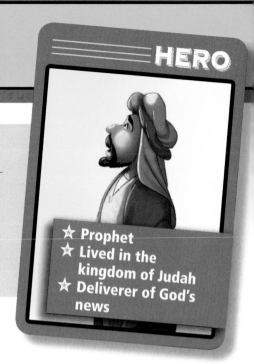

☆ Prophet
☆ Lived in the kingdom of Judah
☆ Deliverer of God's news

ISAIAH received messages from God. Sometimes those messages were warnings—things nobody wanted to hear. Sometimes God's messages were beautiful promises of his love for the people. No matter what the messages were, Isaiah told the people what God wanted them to hear.

One day, Isaiah saw God sitting on a throne wearing a royal robe. Isaiah was frightened, but an angel flew to Isaiah and touched a burning coal to Isaiah's lips. The angel said, "Your sins and guilt are taken away."

Then God asked, "Who should I send as a messenger to my people?"

Isaiah answered, "Send me."

DESTRUCTION AND RESCUE

Isaiah gave people messages from God about all kinds of things—warnings for their country, destruction of their enemies, and news about the Messiah who would save them all. Isaiah scolded his people for the ways they turned away from God. Isaiah offered prayers for his people and promised them that God loved them and wanted to help, comfort, and rescue them.

TO TELL THE TRUTH

No matter what God's messages were, good or bad, Isaiah told the truth. He wanted the Israelite nation to understand who their God was and how much the Lord loved them.

DID YOU KNOW?
Isaiah is quoted over fifty times in the New Testament.

DANIEL

Daniel 1, 4, 6

★ Prophet
★ Advisor to Kings Nebuchadnezzar and Darius of Babylon
★ Thrown into lions' den

BECAUSE Daniel was strong and smart, the king chose Daniel to serve in his palace. The king was pleased with Daniel and gave him more responsibility. But other people weren't always happy with Daniel. No matter what happened to him, good or bad, Daniel continued to love and serve God.

Some of the other officials were jealous of how much the king liked Daniel. They tricked King Darius into signing a law saying that if someone prayed to anyone besides the king, that person would be thrown into the lions' den.

PRAY ANYWAY

Daniel heard about the law but still wanted to talk to God. So even though it could mean death, Daniel prayed to God like he always had.

WHAT HAPPENED IN THE LIONS' DEN?

The king found out and put Daniel in the den of hungry lions. But Daniel trusted God and prayed. God sent an angel to shut the lions' mouths. Daniel was perfectly safe and didn't even have a scratch on him. The next morning the king came to see what happened. Daniel called out, "My God has saved me."

FAITHFUL DANIEL

When Daniel was rewarded, he stayed loyal to God. When Daniel was punished, he remained faithful to God. No matter what happened to Daniel, he stayed true to God and God protected him.

SHADRACH, MESHACH, AND ABEDNEGO

Daniel 3

KING Nebuchadnezzar chose Shadrach, Meshach, and Abednego because of their intelligence, strength, and wisdom to serve in the royal palace. Even though these three young men worked for the powerful king of Babylon, they remained loyal to God.

King Nebuchadnezzar built a giant statue of himself. He ordered everyone to bow down to this statue. But Shadrach, Meshach, and Abednego would not bow down to the statue of the king. Nebuchadnezzar was furious.

NO, THANKS

Nebuchadnezzar gave the three young men one more chance to bow down to his statue or they would be burned in the fiery furnace. Shadrach, Meshach, and Abednego told the king they would never worship a statue. They would only worship God.

THE FIERY FURNACE

So Nebuchadnezzar had his soldiers tie up Shadrach, Meshach, and Abednego and throw them into the furnace. The fire was so hot that the guards who threw them in burned to death. But God protected Shadrach, Meshach, and Abednego.

NOT EVEN HOT

The king saw a fourth man who looked like an angel walking around the blazing furnace with them. Nebuchadnezzar couldn't believe it! The king ordered them out of the fire. Shadrach, Meshach, and Abednego were perfectly fine. They weren't burned or hurt and didn't even smell like smoke!

LOYAL NO MATTER WHAT

Shadrach, Meshach, and Abednego stayed true to God, even when threatened, even when their lives were in danger. God kept these three young men safe.

DID YOU KNOW?

Shadrach, Meshach, and Abednego oversaw all of the business of the province of Babylon.

NEBUCHADNEZZAR

Daniel 2, 4 (also mentioned in Jeremiah; 2 Kings; Ezekiel; and 1 and 2 Chronicles)

VILLAIN

☆ King of Babylon
☆ Became king in 604 BC
☆ Built statue of himself

NEBUCHADNEZZAR was a powerful king of the Babylonian Empire. He believed in God, but repeatedly took credit for his success instead of thanking God for it.

Nebuchadnezzar had a dream of a giant statue. The dream meant that when Nebuchadnezzar was no longer king, other kingdoms would dominate but that God would ultimately rule everything. Nebuchadnezzar praised God as the mightiest.

THE GOLDEN STATUE

But Nebuchadnezzar's pride took over again. He built a statue of himself and forced everyone to bow down to it (pp. 60–61). God showed Nebuchadnezzar that he was stronger than any man ever could be. Nebuchadnezzar went back to worshiping God.

THE CRAZY DREAM

However, Nebuchadnezzar again let his self-importance take over. He had a new dream warning that he'd go crazy and live like an animal, eating grass like a cow! God made this happen to show Nebuchadnezzar who was truly king.

Nebuchadnezzar went crazy for years, just as the dream had predicted. When the time was up, Nebuchadnezzar returned to normal and immediately exclaimed that God deserved all the glory.

BACK AND FORTH

Nebuchadnezzar had moments where he understood how awesome God is, but he continuously struggled to realize that God is mightier than he could ever be.

EZEKIEL

Ezekiel

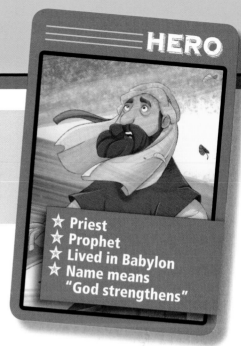
GOD spoke to Ezekiel in visions—fantastic dreams! Ezekiel faithfully followed God's call and did exactly as God instructed him, even when the people wouldn't listen.

In one vision, God gave Ezekiel a scroll to eat. The scroll tasted like honey and had messages for the Israelites on it. God told Ezekiel, "You must give them my messages, whether they listen or not."

DRAW A MAP

The Israelites had turned away from God, but God loved them. God asked Ezekiel to do some crazy things to get the Israelites' attention. God had Ezekiel draw a map of Jerusalem on a brick and build a wall and enemy camp around it to show what the attack on Jerusalem would look like.

LIE DOWN

God asked Ezekiel to lie on his left side for 390 days and then on his right side for forty more days, eating only bread and water to show the Israelites their sins.

DON'T SHAVE

God asked Ezekiel to shave his hair and his beard. Ezekiel did all these things for God. Ezekiel was a great prophet who delivered important messages from God to the Israelites, even when it required going to great lengths.

Ezekiel heard God's voice speaking to him from within a whirlwind (or great storm).

DID YOU KNOW?

God touched the prophet Isaiah's lips with coal and had Ezekiel eat a scroll.

63

ZERUBBABEL

Ezra 1–6; Nehemiah 7

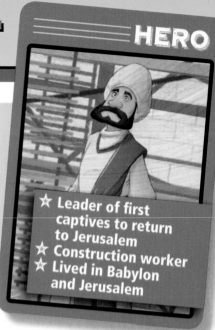

ZERUBBABEL left Persia along with forty-two thousand men to return to Jerusalem and rebuild God's temple that Nebuchadnezzar's army had destroyed. The city was in ruins. Zerubbabel was determined to rebuild the house of the LORD, no matter what it took.

Zerubbabel got permission from the king to leave Babylon and take a crew of construction workers with him. The first thing Zerubbabel and his fellow workers built was an altar so they could give offerings to God. Next they began to build the temple.

TIME TO CELEBRATE

When the foundation was in place, Zerubbabel and all his people rejoiced—singing, playing instruments, and praising God. They were so happy to be back home and be rebuilding their place to worship God.

CONSTRUCTION OFF

But King Artaxerxes didn't want the temple rebuilt since Jerusalem had revolted so many times in the past. He ordered that the work be stopped. The reconstruction of the temple was halted.

CONSTRUCTION ON AGAIN

Zerubbabel and his crew started back up again a few years later when another Persian king gave them permission to continue. Zerubbabel and the workers labored hard for twenty years, until the temple was rebuilt. Even though it was hard work and a powerful king tried to stop it, Zerubbabel and his men were unwavering in rebuilding God's temple.

HAMAN

Esther 3–10

☆ Astrologer
☆ Advisor to King Xerxes of Persia
☆ Schemed to kill all the Jews

HAMAN was the most powerful official in the Persian Empire. But Haman was greedy. He wanted more and more authority, praise, and control, which ended up ruining him.

Because Haman was so high ranking in the king's empire, everyone was supposed to bow down to him to show respect. But one man, Mordecai, refused to bow down to Haman.

REVENGE

This made Haman so furious that he wanted to punish Mordecai (p. 66). When Haman found out that Mordecai wouldn't bow down to him, Haman decided to penalize not just Mordecai, but all the Jews since Mordecai was Jewish. Haman slyly convinced the king to have all the Jewish people killed.

THE QUEEN STEPS IN

But Queen Esther (who happened to be Jewish) exposed Haman's evil plan, and the king put an end to it. King Xerxes also put an end to Haman for scheming to kill the Jews, which would have included the queen.

MORE IS LESS

Haman had so much, but he wanted more. Haman's desire for more power ended up causing him to lose everything. King Xerxes was so angry that he had Haman killed.

I LOVE A PARADE

The king wanted to reward Mordecai for saving the king's life. He went to Haman and asked, "What should I do for someone I'm pleased with?"

Haman thought the king was talking about him. So Haman suggested the king have a parade for this person. "This is what is done for the man the king delights to honor!" he said. When Haman found out the king was talking about Mordecai, that the parade was for Mordecai, he was angry and jealous.

Q: Have you ever watched a parade? What's your favorite thing to see in a parade?

MORDECAI

Esther 2–10

★ Soldier
★ Adopted his cousin Esther
★ Warned of plot to kill King Xerxes

MORDECAI was an honest, loyal man who protected the people he cared about. When Mordecai's aunt and uncle died, he adopted their daughter, Esther (p. 67). When Esther was chosen as queen, Mordecai continued to care for her. Mordecai checked on Esther every day and gave her advice.

Mordecai worked for the king and did his work well, but Mordecai wouldn't bow down to the king's official, Haman (p. 65).

WARN THE KING

One day, Mordecai heard two men saying they wanted to kill the king. Mordecai told Queen Esther about the men's plan. Esther told the king. Together they kept King Xerxes safe.

PROTECT THE JEWS

When Haman decided to kill all the Jews, Mordecai again wanted to protect his people. Mordecai went to Esther and said, "Perhaps you were made queen for just such a time as this." Mordecai convinced Esther to beg the king for the safety of the Jews.

A RESCUER

Mordecai rescued Esther from being an orphan, King Xerxes from being murdered, and the Jews from being destroyed. He did this by standing up for what he believed in and speaking up to keep people safe.

DID YOU KNOW?

King Xerxes threw a parade for Mordecai to thank him for saving his life. The king even let Mordecai wear the king's robe and ride on the king's donkey in the parade.

ESTHER

Esther 2–10

HERO

★ Orphan
★ Queen
★ Wife of King Xerxes
★ Cousin of Mordecai
★ Helped save the Jewish people

ESTHER was a beautiful orphan girl who became queen. She used her courage to save her people.

Esther's parents died when she was a girl. Her cousin Mordecai (p. 66) adopted her.

When King Xerxes was looking for a new queen, he chose Esther out of all the young women in the kingdom. Esther moved to the palace and became Queen Esther of Persia.

A JEW

Esther was Jewish but never told anyone at the palace about her nationality. But when the king's evil advisor, Haman, planned to kill all the Jewish people, Esther knew it was time to speak up. But how?

A HOSTESS

Anyone who talked to the king without an invitation, even the queen, could be killed. Esther was scared, but knew she had to defend her people. So Esther invited King Xerxes to dinner. During dinner, Esther told the king about the scheme to kill her and her people. The king was furious.

A HERO

Esther begged Xerxes to save the Jews. The king put a plan into effect to protect the Jews. The Jewish nation was saved, because Esther was brave enough to risk her life to approach the king and speak for her people.

MARY
MOTHER OF JESUS

Matthew 1–2, 28; Mark 3;
Luke 1–2; John 19

HERO

☆ Mother
☆ Disciple
☆ Mother of Jesus and James
☆ Wife of Joseph

MARY was chosen by God to become the mother of God's Son, Jesus. Although she did not quite understand what this meant, Mary trusted God's wisdom more than her own to parent the Messiah.

When Mary was a teenager, the angel Gabriel told her, "You will have a baby boy and name him Jesus. He will be great, and his kingdom will have no end." Even though this was shocking news, Mary answered, "I'll do whatever God wants me to do."

NO ROOM AT THE INN

When it was time for Mary to have her baby, she and her husband, Joseph, were in Bethlehem, where Joseph's family was from. The town was crowded. There was no room for Mary and Joseph except for where animals were kept. This was not the coziest place to have a baby, but Mary knew God was with her. She had her baby, named him Jesus, and laid him in a manger.

MOTHER AND DISCIPLE

When Jesus grew up, Mary stayed with him. Mary was with Jesus when he performed his first miracle—turning water into wine at a wedding. Mary followed Jesus as he preached about God's kingdom, healed the lame, and gave sight to blind people. Mary stayed faithful to Jesus—even when people challenged him, made fun of him, and eventually killed him.

WITH HIM UNTIL THE END

When Jesus was hung on a cross to die, Mary was there at the foot of the cross, weeping for her son. Mary loved and cared for her son, Jesus, his entire life.

Q: When Mary had Jesus, shepherds came to worship her son. Do you know who came to see you when you were born?

SIMEON AND ANNA

When Jesus was a baby, Mary and Joseph took him to the temple to present him to God. An old man named Simeon saw Jesus and began praising God for allowing him to see the Messiah before he died. Anna, a prophet was also at the temple and praised God when she saw Jesus. Anna told everyone that this child would rescue Jerusalem.

JOSEPH

Matthew 1–2; Luke 2

HERO

★ Carpenter
★ Husband of Mary
★ Lived in Bethlehem and Nazareth

JOSEPH was Mary's husband. He helped look after and protect Jesus. God sent angels to Joseph many times to give him directions. Joseph listened to God's instructions and trusted God's plans.

Before Joseph was married, an angel came to him and said, "Your fiancée, Mary, will have a baby. Name him Jesus. He will save the people from their sins." Joseph did as the angel told him, even though this was something that might have created gossip.

THE ANGEL SAYS . . . MOVE

When Jesus was a toddler, another angel spoke to Joseph in a dream, saying, "King Herod wants to kill Jesus. To protect Jesus, take him and Mary to Egypt." That very night, Joseph took Mary and Jesus, left their home, and moved to the foreign land of Egypt, just as God had instructed.

THE ANGEL SAYS . . . MOVE BACK

When King Herod died, another angel came to Joseph and said it was time to move back to Israel. So Joseph gathered Mary and Jesus and moved them to a town in Israel called Nazareth.

IF YOU SAY SO

No matter what God told him to do, Joseph did it. Joseph trusted God and took care of Jesus in all the ways God asked him to.

THE WISE MEN

Matthew 2

★ Early Scientists
★ Philosophers
★ Astrologists

WISE men from the east saw a special star in the sky and recognized it as the star signaling the Messiah's birth. The wise men followed this star a long distance to find and worship the newborn king.

DID YOU KNOW?

Nobody knows how many wise men there were, but they are often referred to as the "three kings."

The wise men tracked the star to the town of Bethlehem and continued to follow it to where it stopped over a house. They were so happy that the star had led them to the new king! The wise men went into the house and saw Jesus and his mother, Mary, inside.

A JOURNEY

The wise men faithfully followed a star, believing that the star would lead them to the king of the Jews. When they finally saw Jesus, the wise men were overwhelmed with joy.

THE GIFTS

The wise men immediately bowed down to Jesus. They gave him expensive treasures—gifts fit for a king. The wise men worshiped Jesus and were delighted that their long journey had brought them to the promised Messiah.

HEROD THE GREAT

Matthew 2; Luke 1

☆ King of Judea
☆ Builder
☆ Ruled from 37–4 BC

KING Herod was a powerful king of Judea. But Herod let the fear of someone overtaking his throne push him into doing horrible, cruel things.

The Roman government gave Herod the title of "king of the Jews," but the Jewish people did not consider him their Messiah. Herod was not a descendant of King David. He wasn't even fully Jewish. When wise men from the east (p. 71) asked about the newborn king of the Jews, Herod was alarmed. He was suspicious that someone was trying to take his throne.

GET RID OF THE COMPETITION

Herod asked the wise men, "When did you first see the star leading to the Messiah?" He sent them to Bethlehem and told the wise men, "When you find the child, come back and tell me where he is." Herod lied and added, "I want to worship the Messiah, too." Herod didn't want to visit with the baby—he wanted to destroy the child.

BLOCKED PLANS

Herod's evil scheme failed. The wise men did not return, so Herod could not find the child. Instead, he had all the baby boys who had been born since the star first appeared in the sky killed. But Jesus escaped safely to Egypt with his family. Herod died without ever locating the baby Jesus.

DID YOU KNOW?

Herod was known for building things. He rebuilt the beautiful Jewish temple, but he also built many temples for other gods.

JOHN THE BAPTIST

Matthew 3, 11, 14; Mark 1, 6; Luke 1, 3, 7; John 1, 3

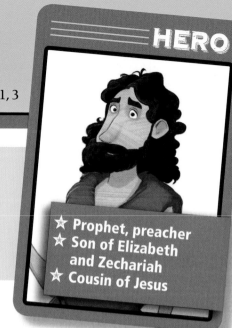

HERO

☆ Prophet, preacher
☆ Son of Elizabeth and Zechariah
☆ Cousin of Jesus

GOD chose John to prepare people for the coming of the Messiah. This was a huge responsibility, but John did not let it go to his head. He remained humble and helped point people to Jesus.

Before John was born, an angel told John's father, Zechariah, that he would have a son who would be filled with the Holy Spirit and would turn many Israelites back to God. As John grew, it was just as the angel predicted. John committed his life to God.

IN THE WILDERNESS

John lived a simple life in the wilderness, wearing rough clothes made of camel hair and eating honey and insects called locusts. People came from all over to hear John preach about God. John urged the people to confess their sins and be baptized to show they were giving their lives back to God.

DID YOU KNOW?

When Mary was pregnant with Jesus, she went to visit her cousin Elizabeth, who was pregnant with John.

SOMEONE BETTER IS COMING

The people loved John, but John didn't want people to pay attention only to him. He wanted people to focus on God. John told the crowds, "Someone is coming who is so much greater than I am. I'm not even worthy to tie his shoes." John was talking about Jesus.

WHO SHOULD BAPTIZE WHOM?

Jesus asked John to baptize him. John knew that Jesus was the Messiah, the one he had been talking about. So John said, "I'm not worthy, Jesus. You should be baptizing me!" Jesus responded, "God wants this to happen." John wanted to obey God, so he did as Jesus asked.

BOLD WORDS

John was bold in speaking God's truth. He didn't care what it cost him to share God's message. John even confronted King Herod about his sin (p. 72).

TRAGIC END

Herod's family had John executed because he had upset them by confronting Herod about his sin. John spent his life telling the crowds about the great Messiah who was coming to change everything. John's preaching helped thousands of people turn back to God.

Bath on the bank of the Jordan River

HEROD ANTIPAS

Matthew 14; Mark 6; Luke 3, 9, 23; Acts 12

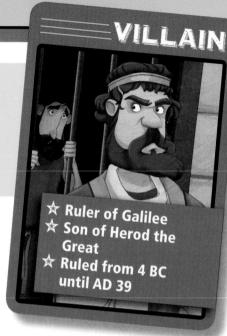

VILLAIN

HEROD Antipas was ruler of Galilee. The messages of John the Baptist and Jesus intrigued Herod, but ultimately, keeping his position was more important to Herod than doing what was right.

☆ Ruler of Galilee
☆ Son of Herod the Great
☆ Ruled from 4 BC until AD 39

John the Baptist (pp. 74–75) accused Herod of being illegally married. Herod recognized that John was a holy man, but Herod's wife, Herodias, was furious that John had brought attention to their sinful marriage. Even though Herod enjoyed listening to John, he had John killed.

JUDGING JESUS

When the priests arrested Jesus, he was brought to Herod to be judged. Herod had heard much about Jesus and was excited to meet him. He even hoped Jesus would perform a miracle. Unable to find Jesus guilty of anything, Herod could have released him. But he sent Jesus back to Pilate to be judged.

COWARDLY RULER

Herod was a ruler. Herod had the power to release both John the Baptist and Jesus. Both men died because Herod would not help them.

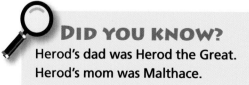

DID YOU KNOW?
Herod's dad was Herod the Great. Herod's mom was Malthace.

The ruins of the palace of King Herod's Masada (in Israel)

CAIAPHAS

Matthew 26; Luke 3; John 11, 18; Acts 4

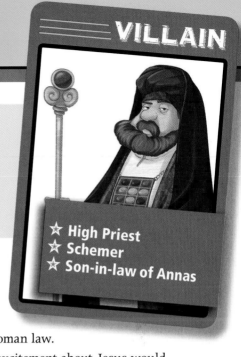

VILLAIN

☆ **High Priest**
☆ **Schemer**
☆ **Son-in-law of Annas**

CAIAPHAS was a devout Jew and the high priest of the Jewish temple. Caiaphas and the other leaders of the temple felt threatened by Jesus and planned to kill him to protect themselves.

The priests knew that the Romans, who ruled over the Jewish people, allowed the Jews to worship their God— but only if the Jews stayed calm and followed Roman law. Caiaphas and the other priests worried that the excitement about Jesus would cause so much of a stir that the Roman army might take away power from the priests and destroy the temple.

ARE YOU THE CHRIST?

Caiaphas and the other priests planned to get rid of Jesus. They found Jesus and had him arrested. Caiaphas and the other religious leaders accused Jesus of blasphemy—saying he was God when he actually wasn't.

Caiaphas asked, "Are you the Christ? The Son of God?"

Jesus answered, "You have said so."

NO PROOF

Even though Caiaphas couldn't prove Jesus had done anything wrong, he was fearful that Jesus's ministry would put his authority in danger. To protect himself, Caiaphas had Jesus arrested, put on trial, and killed.

DID YOU KNOW?
Caiaphas was high priest for eighteen years.

PONTIUS PILATE

Matthew 27; Mark 15; Luke 3, 13, 23; John 18–19

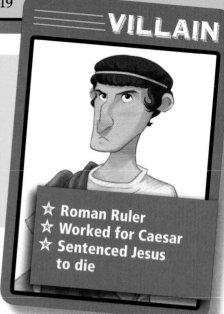

VILLAIN

☆ Roman Ruler
☆ Worked for Caesar
☆ Sentenced Jesus to die

PILATE was a Roman governor. When Jesus was brought in front of him on trial, Pilate had the option to free Jesus or let the Jewish people punish him for a crime he didn't commit. Even though Pilate knew it was wrong, he gave in to the Jews and their false charges.

The high priests wanted Jesus killed but didn't have the authority to sentence someone to death. So they brought Jesus to the ruler who could command execution—Pontius Pilate. Pilate believed that Jesus hadn't done anything wrong. He told the Jews to judge him themselves. But the Jewish priests pushed back. They wanted Pilate to judge Jesus.

DO YOU WANT TO LET HIM GO?

Pilate said, "I release one prisoner for you each year during this feast. Should it be Jesus?" The religious leaders wanted someone else.

Again, Pilate said, "I don't find Jesus guilty." But the crowd cried out to have Jesus crucified. Pilate said, "He's your king. Do what you want."

PEER PRESSURE

Pilate was amazed by Jesus's peace and honesty. Pilate believed that Jesus was innocent and repeatedly tried to release him. Eventually, Pilate gave in and let the crowd have their way.

DID YOU KNOW?

As Pilate was trying to decide what to do with Jesus, he got a message from his wife. She said, "Leave Jesus alone. He is innocent. I had a troubling dream about him."

BARABBAS

Matthew 27; Mark 15; Luke 23; John 18

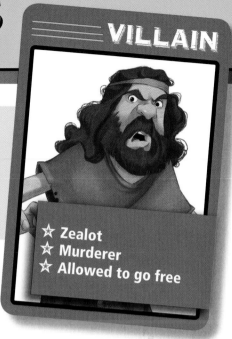

VILLAIN

☆ Zealot
☆ Murderer
☆ Allowed to go free

BARABBAS was a rebel who committed murder at a riot. He was arrested and sentenced to be executed for his crime. Despite what he had done, Barabbas was set free by the government.

Barabbas disliked the way the Romans ruled the Jewish people. He was at an uprising against the Romans and killed someone on that day. He was put in prison for what he had done.

GET-OUT-OF-JAIL-FREE CARD

There was a tradition that each year, at the feast of Passover, one Jewish prisoner would be set free. The government was deciding if they should release Barabbas or another prisoner—Jesus.

FREE MAN

The priests riled up the crowd, trying to convince them to have Barabbas released. Even though everyone knew Barabbas was guilty of murder, they chose to free him. Barabbas was let go, and Jesus was crucified.

DID YOU KNOW?

Today, someone like Barabbas would be in the news. In the United States, he would go to trial for a judge to decide if he was guilty or innocent and to decide what his punishment should be.

The Roman prison cell Barabbas was kept in before he was released

JUDAS ISCARIOT

Matthew 10, 26–27; Mark 3, 14; Luke 6, 22; John 6, 12–13, 18; Acts 1

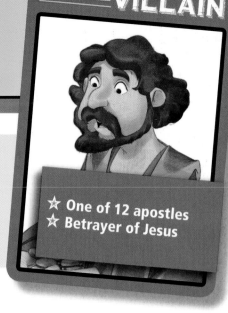

VILLAIN

☆ One of 12 apostles
☆ Betrayer of Jesus

JUDAS Iscariot was one of Jesus's friends and disciples. Judas traveled and lived with Jesus for three years. Judas loved Jesus, but Judas sold out his dear friend for a bag of silver.

Judas was one of the twelve men Jesus chose to be his closest companions— his disciples, or apostles. Judas was put in charge of keeping the money for the disciples. Sometimes Judas stole some of the money for himself.

A BOTTLE OF PERFUME

One day, one of Jesus's friends, Mary, used an entire bottle of expensive perfume on Jesus. "We should have sold that perfume and given the money to the poor," Judas complained. But Judas was actually upset because he couldn't steal any of that money for himself.

A BAG OF SILVER

When the chief priests were scheming to catch Jesus, Judas went to them and agreed to betray his friend for a bag of silver. A few days later, Judas led a crowd of religious leaders to the garden where Jesus was praying.

Q: Have you ever asked someone to hold or keep your money for you?

A KISS

Judas kissed Jesus to show the crowd which person they should arrest. Judas was one of Jesus's closest friends, but he betrayed Jesus. He took money to help the high priests arrest Jesus.

DID YOU KNOW?

Judas received thirty pieces of silver from the high priests. Judas took the silver in exchange for helping the high priests catch Jesus, much like Delilah took silver in exchange for helping the Philistines capture Samson.

JOSEPH OF ARIMATHEA

Matthew 27; Mark 15; Luke 23; John 19

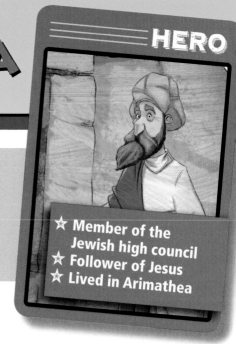

HERO

☆ Member of the Jewish high council
☆ Follower of Jesus
☆ Lived in Arimathea

JOSEPH was a rich man who followed Jesus. Joseph couldn't stop the priests from crucifying Jesus, but Joseph did what he could to care for the body of Jesus.

Joseph was on the religious council, but he did not agree with the high priests. Joseph believed that Jesus was the Messiah. When Jesus was crucified on the cross, Joseph went to Pilate and asked for Jesus's body. Pilate agreed.

I HAVE A TOMB

Joseph took Jesus's body and wrapped it in expensive linen cloth. He laid Jesus in a tomb he had purchased. Joseph rolled a stone in front of the opening of the tomb to keep Jesus's body safe.

I'LL TAKE CARE OF IT

Joseph couldn't save Jesus from being killed, but he could make sure Jesus's body was treated with respect. Joseph used his own money to pay for a proper burial for Jesus.

DID YOU KNOW?

The Gospel of Mark mentions that a man named Nicodemus went with Joseph to get Jesus's body and put it in the tomb.

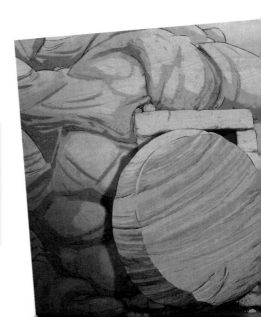

MARTHA AND MARY

Luke 10; John 11

★ Sisters
★ Homemakers
★ Brother: Lazarus
★ Followers of Jesus

MARY and Martha loved each other, their brother Lazarus, and Jesus. And although they were similar in many ways, like most sisters, Mary and Martha sometimes had different ideas of what was most important.

One day, when Jesus visited, Martha stayed busy preparing food to please Jesus. Meanwhile, Mary sat listening to Jesus teach. Both women thought they were doing the right thing.

I BELIEVE

When Mary and Martha's brother, Lazarus, died, the sisters were miserable. Days later, Jesus came to see them. Martha ran to Jesus saying, "Lord, if you had been here, Lazarus wouldn't have died." Jesus answered, "Everyone who believes in me will live forever. Do you believe that?" Martha answered, "I have always believed you are the Messiah."

SOMETIMES THE SAME

Mary came outside, telling Jesus the same thing, "Lord, if you had been here, Lazarus wouldn't have died." Jesus cried and called, "Where is he?" Jesus went to the tomb and told Lazarus to come out. Lazarus, who had died, walked out of his tomb!

BOTH BELIEVERS

Mary and Martha both loved Jesus. Martha thought the best way to please Jesus was by serving him. Mary wanted to learn as much as she could from Jesus. The sisters believed that Jesus was the Messiah and followed him in their own ways.

MARY MAGDALENE

Matthew 27–28; Mark 15–16; Luke 8, 24; John 19–20

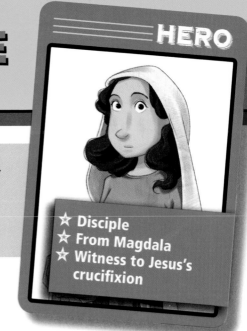

HERO

☆ Disciple
☆ From Magdala
☆ Witness to Jesus's crucifixion

FOLLOWING Jesus changed Mary Magdalene's life. Being associated with Jesus was dangerous, but Jesus was more important to Mary than playing it safe.

When Jesus died, Mary Magdalene was there, even though anyone supporting Jesus might get arrested. Early Sunday, Mary Magdalene again risked her safety for Jesus. She was the first one at the tomb where he had been laid.

EMPTY TOMB

Mary was alarmed to see the tomb empty. She was sad that Jesus had died and was even more upset to see that he was gone. Mary Magdalene ran back to tell the other followers that someone had taken Jesus's body.

HOW COULD YOU BE HERE?

She returned to the tomb crying. Jesus appeared behind her, but Mary wasn't expecting him to be standing there. She thought he was dead! Then Mary recognized Jesus. Jesus told Mary to tell the others what she'd seen.

GUESS WHAT I SAW

Mary Magdalene was eager to share the news that Jesus was alive. She ran back to tell the disciples, "I've seen the Lord." Mary Magdalene was devoted to Jesus. She took risks to share everything she knew about Jesus with others.

DID YOU KNOW?
Other women who may have gone to the tomb early Sunday morning with Mary Magdalene were Salome, Mary (James's mother), and Joanna.

HEROD AGRIPPA

Acts 25–26

VILLAIN

HEROD Agrippa was a ruler who did terrible things to some members of the church. He tried to get the apostle Paul in trouble. He loved power and praise and ignored all that God had provided for him.

☆ Ruler
☆ Grandson of Herod the Great
☆ Ruled from AD 41–44

Herod had the apostle James (p. 95) killed for being a Christian. The Jewish people seemed happy that Herod had executed a disciple, so he threw Peter (p. 94) in jail with plans to kill him too. But an angel helped Peter escape. Herod was so angry his scheme had failed that he had all the soldiers guarding Peter killed.

ALL DRESSED UP

While making peace with neighboring cities, Herod put on his fancy robes, sat on his throne, and gave a speech. The people were impressed with Herod in all his finery and shouted, "It's the voice of a god, not a man!" Herod could give credit to God or let the people worship him. Herod chose to let the people worship him.

CURSED

Herod loved the attention but was instantly cursed for this mistake with a sickness that killed him. He was so caught up in gaining praise that he failed to recognize God. Herod killed and jailed innocent men just to make the crowds like him. His horrible decisions ended his life.

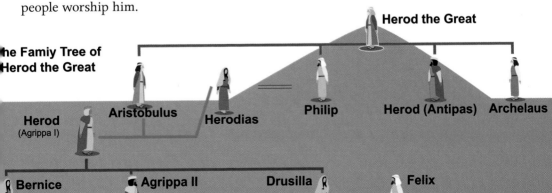

The Family Tree of Herod the Great

Herod the Great

Herod (Agrippa I)

Aristobulus

Herodias

Philip

Herod (Antipas)

Archelaus

Bernice

Agrippa II

Drusilla

Felix

BARNABAS

Acts 4, 9, 11–15; 1 Corinthians 9:6; Galatians 2

BARNABAS helped spread the good news of Jesus after Jesus went to heaven. Barnabas's friends gave him the nickname "encourager," because he cheered for the people around him even when no one else would.

HERO
- ☆ Missionary
- ☆ Cousin of John Mark
- ☆ Traveled with Paul

Paul (p. 108) had a dangerous past, and many of the existing Christians feared that Paul would hurt them. But Barnabas took the risk to get to know Paul and discovered that he was a changed man. Barnabas convinced the apostles that they could now trust Paul.

YOU'LL LOVE JESUS

When Paul and Barnabas traveled to Antioch, Barnabas was so happy to meet the Christians there. Barnabas was strong in his faith and encouraged the people to stay true to Jesus.

Monastery of St. Barnabas, Northern Cyprus

I LIKE JOHN MARK

Paul and John Mark (p. 88) got in a disagreement. When it was time to sail to another city to tell more people about Jesus, Paul didn't want John Mark to come along. But Barnabas stood up for John Mark. He told Paul to take the trip where he was headed, and he would go with John Mark to spread the word about Jesus in other cities.

WHAT A GOOD FRIEND

Barnabas was a good man who wanted others to know about Jesus. Barnabas stood up for others, even when it meant challenging the people he cared about.

DID YOU KNOW?
Barnabas's real name was Joseph, but his nickname was Barnabas, which means "son of encouragement."

SILAS

Acts 15

HERO

★ Missionary
★ Jailed with Paul

SILAS devoted his life to spreading the news of Jesus. This meant traveling to foreign places, being thrown in jail, and even risking his life. But Silas wasn't shaken. He stayed focused on his work.

Silas traveled with Paul (p. 108), telling crowds about Jesus. They were repeatedly threatened and chased out of towns for their preaching. While in Philippi, they were beaten and thrown in jail. Even in a dungeon, Silas and Paul sang and prayed out loud.

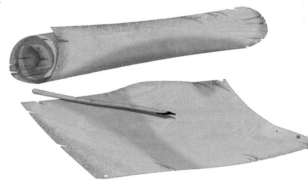

SAVING THE JAILER

Suddenly, an earthquake caused the doors to fly open and the prisoners' chains to fall off. The jailer knew he would be punished if the prisoners escaped. But when he turned on the lights and saw everyone still there, the jailer was amazed. He asked Silas and Paul, "How can I be saved?" Silas and Paul told the jailer that if he believed in Jesus, he and his whole family would be saved. The jailer believed, and Silas and Paul were set free.

A LIFE OF DANGER

Silas's life was filled with danger, but he thought sharing the news about Jesus was more important than being safe.

Q: Do you have a favorite song you like to sing when you're scared or in trouble?

JOHN MARK

Acts 12–15

JOHN Mark wanted to tell people about Jesus. But early in his travels, he gave up. When he was given a second chance to spread Christianity, John Mark took it.

John Mark, also known as Mark, was chosen to sail with Paul (p. 108) and Barnabas (p. 86) to Cyprus. In Cyprus they taught the word of God in the Jewish synagogues. On the second stop of their trip, John Mark left Paul and Barnabas and returned to Jerusalem. This angered Paul. He and John Mark had a nasty argument.

A SECOND TRIP

When Paul was planning a second trip, Barnabas wanted to bring John Mark with them. But Paul was still angry and wouldn't let John Mark come. So Paul went his own way without either of them.

SECOND CHANCES

Barnabas gave John Mark a second chance, and together they returned to Cyprus. John Mark and Barnabas shared with the people all about Jesus. Later in life, John Mark made up with Paul, and they became friends.

SECOND TIME AROUND

John Mark gave up on being a missionary after only his first stop. With the help of Barnabas, John Mark was encouraged to keep trying and to continue telling people about Jesus.

DID YOU KNOW?

According to some scholars, Mark was dragged by a rope through the streets of Alexandria, Egypt, until he died.

APOLLOS

Acts 18–19; 1 Corinthians 4, 16; Titus 3

HERO

APOLLOS was a fantastic speaker. He explained things well, and people loved listening to him. When he didn't have all his facts straight, Apollos was willing to learn from others.

★ Speaker
★ Missionary
★ Contemporary of Paul

Apollos arrived in Ephesus and started teaching people about Jesus. The crowds gathered and were eager to hear him speak. But Apollos didn't know everything about Jesus. Two Christians in Ephesus—Priscilla and Aquila—met with Apollos to share with him the parts of Jesus's ministry and promises he didn't know. Apollos could have gotten mad at them for correcting him. Instead, Apollos listened to Priscilla and Aquila and was grateful for the extra knowledge. In fact, with this additional information, Apollos was now even more excited to share about Jesus.

LIFE LEARNER

Apollos took the things he already knew about the Bible and Jesus, plus the facts Priscilla and Aquila shared with him, to spread the news that Jesus was the Messiah. He used his talent for speaking to do this, but he also accepted the help of others to share Christianity.

Q: What do you like to learn about?

PETER

The four Gospels and Acts

HERO

★ Fisherman
★ Apostle
★ Church Leader

PETER was a simple fisherman who was called by Jesus to do great things. This doesn't mean Peter was perfect. He had a temper and wanted things to go his way. But Peter loved Jesus enough to do what was important to Jesus.

One day while Peter was fishing, Jesus said, "Follow me." Peter didn't ask questions. He dropped his fishing nets and followed Jesus.

WALKING ON WATER

Another time Jesus was walking on the sea toward the disciples. They were astounded. Peter called, "Jesus, if that's you, call me to walk on water too."

Jesus said, "Come." Peter went toward Jesus. He was walking on water! Then a gust of wind frightened Peter. Peter began to sink, but Jesus rescued him and encouraged Peter to have more faith.

YOU ARE THE CHRIST

Peter spent three years with Jesus. He listened to Jesus teach about the kingdom of God, witnessed him perform miracles, and even saw Jesus transformed into his radiant godly image. Peter proclaimed out loud to Jesus, "You are the Christ."

THE ROOSTER

Before he was arrested, Jesus warned Peter that he would deny Jesus before the rooster crowed the next morning. Peter argued that he would never deny Jesus. But Jesus was right. Peter was so worried about what might happen to him that when people asked if he knew Jesus, he lied and said, "I don't know him."

AN ASSIGNMENT FROM JESUS

Days after Jesus rose from the dead, he made breakfast for the disciples. Even though Peter had made mistakes, Jesus still loved him. Jesus told Peter to take care of his people.

ORDINARY AND EXTRAORDINARY

Peter wasn't rich, important, or famous. He was moody and made mistakes sometimes. But Peter chose to follow Jesus. And because Jesus knew how faithful Peter was, he gave Peter the responsibility of being in charge of the church.

DID YOU KNOW?

Peter's original name was Simon, but Jesus changed it to Peter, which means "rock."

STEPHEN

Acts 6–8

HERO

STEPHEN understood that Jesus was the Messiah who would save the Jewish people. Stephen did everything he could, no matter what the cost, to share this truth with others.

☆ Disciple
☆ Kitchen Help
☆ First Martyr
☆ Died around AD 34

Stephen could perform great miracles and show signs. Some Jewish men felt threatened by Stephen's message and acts. They wanted to get rid of him.

FALSELY CHARGED

These men lied and said Stephen had claimed that Jesus would destroy their temple and the laws of Moses. When he was blamed for this thing he didn't do, Stephen didn't get defensive or upset. Instead, his face glowed like an angel's.

HISTORY OF THE JEWS

Stephen knew the history of the Jewish people and spoke to them about Abraham, Joseph, Moses, King David, and King Solomon. Stephen shared that again and again the Jewish people had turned away from God. He told the crowds that Jesus was the Messiah that God had promised long ago. Stephen warned the Jews that they were still turning away from God.

DID YOU KNOW?

Stephen was picked with six other men to help pass out food to the early church.

YOU DON'T SCARE ME

The crowd was furious that Stephen would accuse them of not being faithful to God.

But the angry crowd didn't startle or frighten Stephen. He looked to heaven and saw Jesus. He told the crowd, "Look, I see Jesus at God's right hand!" Still, the people wouldn't listen. They grabbed Stephen and stoned him to death.

CERTAINTY

Stephen didn't allow others to trouble or confuse him. He was sure of who Jesus was and did everything he could to let others know the truth. Stephen was the first person mentioned in the Bible to die proclaiming Jesus as Messiah.

Q: Do you ever help get a meal ready for your family?

LUKE

Acts 16–28

JESUS was so important to Luke that he decided to write a detailed account of both Jesus's life and the early church. Luke said he was doing this so people would know the truth.

Luke and the apostle Paul (p. 108) were close companions who traveled together sharing the good news. In Paul's second letter to Timothy, he says, "Luke is the only one with me." In Paul's letter to the Colossians, he calls Luke, "beloved doctor." Paul's letter to Philemon names Luke as his "fellow worker."

HOW LUKE SHARED WHAT HE KNEW

Jesus changed Luke's life, and Luke in turn spent his life helping people understand who Jesus was. Luke did this both by being a missionary with Paul and by writing a biography of Jesus and a history of the early church. And since Luke was a doctor, he describes the miraculous healings Jesus performed with more medical details than some of the other gospel writers. Some of these healings include; healing Peter's mother-in-law's fever, making a paralyzed man walk, stopping the bleeding of a woman who had bled for twelve years, and raising the widow's son and a little girl from the dead.

Q: Do you like to write or draw pictures about things that happened to you or the people you know?

Ancient doctor or surgeon's tool kit

JAMES
BROTHER OF JOHN
The four Gospels and Acts

☆ Fisherman
☆ Apostle
☆ Brother of John
☆ Cousin of Jesus

JAMES was in Jesus's inner circle, along with Peter and John. They were the people closest to Jesus during his three years of ministry. James was devoted to Jesus and would endure anything for him.

One day, James was in a fishing boat with his father and his younger brother, John. Jesus called to them. James and John immediately followed him, leaving their boat, their father, and their old lives behind.

CAN I SIT NEXT TO YOU?

James and John wanted to be close to Jesus always. One day James and John asked Jesus, "When you sit on your throne, can one of us sit on each side of you?"

Jesus said, "You don't know what you're asking! Can you handle the bitterness I'll have to face?"

"Oh, yes," James and John answered. Jesus said they would have to handle the same bitterness he would, but that it wasn't his choice who could sit on his right and left.

I WANT TO BE WITH YOU

The moment James met Jesus, he knew he wanted to be with him— no matter what. James left his job and his family to follow Jesus. Later, Herod Agrippa (p. 85) had James killed because he was a follower of Jesus. James willingly accepted suffering and eventually died because of his loyalty to Jesus.

DID YOU KNOW?

Jesus nicknamed John and his brother, James, "Sons of Thunder."

JOHN

John 1–21; Matthew; Mark; Luke; Acts 1

HERO

JOHN heard and saw remarkable things from Jesus. He believed with his whole heart that Jesus was the Messiah. Some think that John called himself the disciple Jesus loved.

★ Apostle
★ Fisherman
★ Brother of James
★ Cousin of Jesus

John and his brother were disciples of John the Baptist (p. 74). One day, they were standing with the John the Baptist as Jesus walked by. John the Baptist said, "Look, there is the Lamb of God!" This was an incredible statement. The man who had been teaching John about God said Jesus was God!

DISCIPLESHIP

John and his brother, James, began following Jesus. John ate with Jesus, prayed with Jesus, watched Jesus heal people, and listened to Jesus teach. John became one of his closest friends and was included in Jesus's inner circle (along with Peter and James).

THE TRANSFIGURATION

When John, James, and Peter went up a mountain with Jesus, Jesus completely transformed and turned a dazzling white before their eyes. A voice from heaven said, "This is my beloved Son, listen to him."

HEARD THEM SAY IT

John heard his teacher proclaim that Jesus was the Lamb of God, and God himself announced that Jesus was his Son. John was completely convinced that Jesus would save the world. After Jesus ascended into heaven, John committed his life to telling as many people as possible about Jesus.

The Bible tells us that John was exiled to the island of Patmos.

MATTHEW

Matthew 9–10; Mark 3; Luke 6; Acts 1

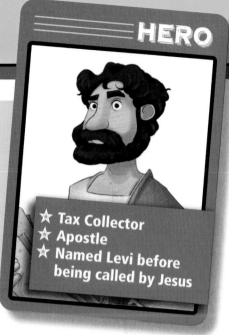

HERO

MATTHEW was a tax collector. This meant Matthew was rich, but it also likely meant he cheated and stole money, taking more than his share. When he met Jesus, Matthew had a decision to make. Would Matthew continue in his old life or would he change his ways?

★ Tax Collector
★ Apostle
★ Named Levi before being called by Jesus

One day, while Matthew was working at his tax-collecting booth, Jesus said, "Follow me." This meant Matthew would have to give up his wealth. But he did it. Matthew got up and followed Jesus.

DINNER PARTY

Soon after, Matthew invited Jesus and his disciples over for dinner. The religious leaders turned up their noses. They asked Jesus why he was eating with second-rate people. Jesus replied that he had come to help those who needed him.

IN WITH THE NEW

Matthew walked away from a life of luxury and, maybe, cheating. By pursuing Jesus, he gained a great friend and teacher.

DID YOU KNOW?

Grown-ups today pay taxes to the government. Back in Matthew's time, the tax collectors came to your house and took what a family owed the government. Some of them also took whatever extra they wanted for themselves.

THOMAS

Matthew 10; Mark 3; Luke 6; John 11, 14, 20; Acts 1

HERO

☆ Apostle
☆ Missionary
☆ From Galilee

THOMAS was one of Jesus's faithful disciples. When Jesus died, Thomas was miserable. The other disciples claimed Jesus was alive, but it took a miracle for Thomas to believe.

After Jesus was crucified, he appeared to his disciples. Jesus showed the disciples where the nails had pierced his hands and feet. Jesus talked to the disciples and filled them with peace. But Thomas wasn't there.

DOUBTING THOMAS

The other disciples told Thomas they'd seen Jesus—that he was alive! Thomas didn't believe them. Thomas said he couldn't accept that Jesus had come back to life unless he saw and touched Jesus himself.

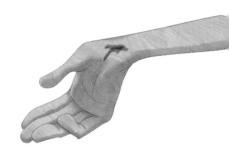

PROOF

Eight days later, Jesus visited the disciples again. This time Thomas was there. Jesus knew Thomas's doubts, went over to Thomas, and said, "Touch my wounds. Don't doubt anymore. Believe that I am alive."

CONVINCED

Thomas was amazed! "My Lord and my God!" he said. Although at first Thomas didn't believe that Jesus had risen from the dead, after he saw Jesus with his own eyes, he was convinced.

DID YOU KNOW?
Thomas's nickname was "the twin."

PHILIP

Matthew 10; Mark 3:18; John 1; Acts 8:4–8, 26–40

★ Apostle
★ Missionary

GOD sent Philip to unexpected places to teach the gospel. He was one of the first disciples to leave Jerusalem. Philip faithfully studied the Bible and went to Samaria and beyond, teaching people about Jesus.

One day, God told Philip to take a desert road. Philip didn't know why but he went. While on the road, Philip saw a eunuch, a man who was high up in the Queen of Ethiopia's court. The man was in his carriage reading the book of Isaiah (p. 58). The Holy Spirit nudged Philip to approach the man. Philip asked, "Do you understand what you're reading?" The eunuch answered, "I need someone to explain it."

GOOD PLACE FOR A BAPTISM

Philip explained that the prophecies the eunuch was reading were about Jesus.

They drove near some water, and the eunuch asked Philip to baptize him. Philip baptized him right there. When they arose from the water, the Holy Spirit grabbed Philip and took him to another town. The eunuch praised God for the experience.

WHERE DID HE GO?

God sent Philip to all kinds of unexpected places:

- Samaria
- Down a desert road
- A town in Judea

In all these places, Philip proclaimed that Jesus was the Messiah.

Q: Have you ever gone somewhere unexpected? How did it make you feel?

ANDREW

Matthew 4, 10; Mark 1, 3, 13; Luke 6; John 1, 6, 12; Acts 1

HERO

★ Apostle
★ Fisherman
★ Brother of Peter

ANDREW was a fisherman who was always looking for ways to solve problems. When Andrew heard Jesus teach, he thought Jesus could change the world. Andrew wanted to learn more about Jesus, so he found his brother Peter (p. 90), and said, "Come on." Andrew and Peter both became disciples of Jesus.

One day, Jesus was on a mountain. A large crowd came toward Jesus and his disciples to hear Jesus teach. Jesus asked one disciple, "Where can we buy bread for these people?"

The disciple answered, "We don't have enough money to feed this crowd." But Andrew chimed in with an idea.

TWO FISH AND FIVE LOAVES

Andrew found a boy with two fish and five loaves of bread. Andrew told Jesus, "Here's some food, even though it's not much for so many people." Jesus blessed the small basket of food and fed thousands of people with it!

LET'S START HERE

Andrew followed Jesus because he was hopeful that Jesus would save the world.

Q: How many people do you think five loaves of bread and two fish would normally feed?

NATHANAEL

Matthew 10; Mark 3; Luke 6; John 1; Acts 1, 21

HERO

★ Apostle
★ Missionary
★ Also called Bartholomew

NATHANAEL had doubts. When he didn't believe or understand something, he asked good questions. Nathanael's curiosity helped him find Jesus, which changed his life forever.

Nathanael's friend Philip told Nathanael, "We have found the man who Moses and the prophets wrote about. His name is Jesus from Nazareth."

Nathanael couldn't imagine that the promised Messiah would come from a place like Nazareth. But he was curious, so he asked Philip, "What good could come from Nazareth?" Philip told Nathanael to come see for himself, and Nathanael went with Philip.

HOW DO YOU KNOW?

Jesus greeted Nathanael and said, "You're a true Israelite. You're an honest man." Nathanael was curious. He'd never even met Jesus. How could he know about his heritage and personality? Nathanael asked, "How do you know about me?"

Jesus told Nathanael he'd seen him under the fig tree before Philip found Nathanael.

HOW DID YOU KNOW ABOUT THE TREE?

How could this be? Jesus knew where Nathanael had been! Jesus's answers convinced Nathanael. He said, "You are the King of Israel." When Nathanael wasn't sure about something, he asked questions. By inquiring about Jesus, Nathanael became one of Jesus's twelve apostles.

JAMES ALPHAEUS, THADDAEUS, AND SIMON THE ZEALOT

Matthew 10; Mark 3; Luke 6; Acts 1

HEROES

★ Apostles
★ Missionaries

JESUS called twelve men to be his main students, his disciples. Each man could decide if he wanted to follow or not. James, son of Alphaeus; Thaddaeus; and Simon the Zealot were three men who chose to be part of this special group of twelve.

Jesus gave his twelve disciples the power to heal the sick, cast out demons, and raise the dead in the name of God. Jesus instructed the twelve to tell the Jewish people the kingdom of heaven was at hand. James of Alphaeus, Thaddaeus, and Simon the Zealot received these abilities and were given these directions from Jesus himself.

WITNESSES TO MIRACLES

Thaddaeus; James, son of Alphaeus; and Simon the Zealot saw Jesus forgive people of their sins, enable the lame to walk, and heal lepers of their skin diseases. James, Simon, and Thaddaeus ate at the Last Supper with Jesus the night before he was arrested. They saw Jesus when he appeared to the disciples after he rose from the dead.

DID YOU KNOW?

James Alphaeus was sometimes referred to as "James the lesser." There could be two reasons for this:
1. Because not much is known about him compared to the other James, or
2. Because he was younger than the other James.

JESUS'S FOLLOWERS

Simon, James, and
Thaddaeus decided to follow
Jesus. As a result, they not
only witnessed miracles and
heard inspiring teaching,
but they also were given
the opportunity to perform
miracles and share the
messages Jesus taught.

MATTHIAS

Acts 1

HERO

★ Disciple
★ Chosen to replace Judas as one of 12 apostles
★ Missionary

WHEN Jesus selected the twelve men who would be his closest disciples, Matthias wasn't chosen. But Matthias didn't get angry or jealous. He wasn't discouraged. Instead, Matthias continued to follow Jesus. Matthias was Jesus's faithful student from the day Jesus was baptized by John the Baptist (pp. 74–75) until the day Jesus was crucified.

The twelve disciples needed to replace Judas after he betrayed Jesus and died (pp. 80–81). The disciples were looking for a man who had been loyal to Jesus throughout his entire ministry. They were looking for a man who was willing to step into the role of apostle. Matthias, who had been faithful all along, was chosen.

Sticks were often used for casting of lots—Mathias received the small stick and was chosen to replace Judas.

DID YOU KNOW?

When looking for a replacement for Judas, the disciples first nominated two men: Matthias and Joseph. They chose Matthias.

REWARDED FOR FAITHFULNESS

Matthias's loyalty and commitment to Jesus was noticed. Matthias was rewarded by being selected from a group of great men to join the other eleven disciples in their ministry.

ANANIAS AND SAPPHIRA

Acts 5

A MARRIED couple named Ananias and Sapphira decided to sell some land they owned and give the money to the church. This was a generous act. But before they donated the money, Ananias and Sapphira agreed to keep some of it for themselves. The couple lied and said they were donating all of the money, even though they weren't.

Ananias brought the money and his lie to Peter (pp. 90–91). Peter said, "That land was yours. You could have kept it. And when you sold it, you could have kept the money or given some or all of it away. Why did you lie about it? You lied to God." Ananias instantly fell to the ground dead.

SHE LIES

Three hours later, Sapphira arrived. She told the same lie to Peter as Ananias had. Immediately, she also fell to the floor dead.

A BAD PLAN

Ananias and Sapphira planned to be dishonest so they could have more money, but it ended up costing them dearly.

Q: Have you ever sold something? What did you do with the money?

SIMON THE SORCERER

Acts 8

☆ Sorcerer or magician
☆ Fake Disciple
☆ Tried to buy God's power

SIMON was a sorcerer in Samaria. He loved all the attention he got for the tricks he performed. Simon thought he could buy God's power to gain more applause from the crowds.

Large crowds in Samaria were gathering to hear a man named Philip (page 99) teach about Jesus. Simon wanted to see why everyone was so interested in Philip. Simon started listening to Philip too. He was even baptized. What Simon liked best about Philip were the signs and miracles Philip performed. They were amazing.

I WANT THAT TOO

Peter and John came to Samaria to help Philip spread Jesus's message. Peter and John laid hands on the believers Philip had baptized so they could receive the Holy Spirit. Simon loved all the praise he got when he performed tricks, and he wanted to be able to give people the Holy Spirit too. Imagine how people would notice him then!

HOW MUCH DOES IT COST?

Simon begged Peter to let him buy this power. Peter explained that you couldn't purchase the ability to give people the Holy Spirit. Only God and the people God chose to work through could do that. Simon pretended he was drawing close to Jesus. But he was actually seeking more attention.

Q: Have you ever been to a magic show or seen someone perform a magic trick? Did you learn how the trick was done?

SAUL OF TARSUS

Acts 7–8

VILLAIN

★ Pharisee
★ Tentmaker
★ Later called Paul

SAUL was a well-educated, dedicated Jew, who was also a citizen of Rome. But Saul was so concerned about protecting the Jewish faith that he was blind to his own wicked decisions.

Saul believed in God and in God's laws passed down from Moses. So he was concerned about a group of people called Christians. These Christians claimed that Jesus was the Son of God. Saul was furious that anyone would question the way the Jewish people had always done things. He set out to destroy anyone who claimed to be a Christian.

STEPHEN'S STONING

Saul was there at the death of Stephen, the first killing of a Christian in the Bible (pp. 92–93). After Stephen was killed, Saul went through the neighborhoods grabbing men and women who were Christians and throwing them in jail.

COULDN'T SEE

Saul believed in God but had his eyes set so firmly on what he already knew about God that he missed seeing the new things God was doing.

🔍 **DID YOU KNOW?**
God later changed Saul's name to Paul.

PAUL

Acts 9–28; Galatians 1–2 (and 12 other letters)

HERO

★ Missionary
★ Preacher
★ Writer

PAUL was the Pharisee also known as Saul (p. 107). He was focused on putting an end to the Christians. Then Paul met Jesus, and this changed everything! From then on, instead of punishing Christians, Paul dedicated his life to proclaiming Jesus as Lord!

One day, Saul was walking down a road to Damascus in search of Christians he could throw in jail. Suddenly a flash like lightning came from the sky, and Saul fell to the ground. A voice from heaven called to Saul, "Why are you persecuting me?"

"Who are you?" Saul asked.

"I am Jesus. Now get up and you'll be told what to do."

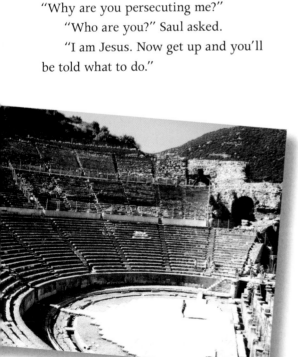

BLINDED BY THE LIGHT

Saul stood and realized he had been blinded. The people he'd been traveling with guided him to Damascus. Saul sat there blind for three days. Not eating. Not drinking. Then a man showed up who said God had sent him to find Saul.

BUT NOW I SEE

The man touched Saul's eyes, and scales fell from his eyes. Saul could see— both with his eyes and with his heart. Not long after that, Saul was called by his other name, "Paul." Paul now understood what Jesus was trying to tell him! He got up, was baptized, and turned his life around. He went out and told anyone who would listen that Jesus was the Son of God.

MAP OF MEDITERRANEAN SHOWING MISSIONARY JOURNEYS

A WHOLE NEW LIFE

Paul traveled around the world taking all kinds of risks to tell people about Jesus. He sent letters to the early churches encouraging them in their Christian faith. Paul was called names, chased, threatened, shipwrecked, put in jail, and eventually killed because of his loyalty to Jesus.

TRANSFORMED

Paul went from prosecuting Christians to becoming one of the most influential and passionate Christian teachers who ever lived.

DID YOU KNOW?
Paul took three missionary journeys to places like modern-day Turkey and Italy, spreading the news of Jesus.

JAMES

James 1–5

JAMES'S parents were Mary (pp. 68–69) and Joseph (p. 70). He grew up with Jesus but didn't understand that Jesus was the Son of God until after Jesus rose from the dead. James taught others the importance of talking to God, putting God first, and staying close to God.

★ Disciple
★ Leader of the church in Jerusalem
★ Son of Mary and Joseph
★ Brother of Jesus

James knew that life wasn't always easy. He wanted people to understand that when things became difficult, you should talk to God. According to some people, James wrote a letter to the early church encouraging Christians to pray about everything. His letter reminded the church to use words wisely and to inspire others. He also reminded people not to judge each other.

HIS LETTER

James was passionate about the teachings of Jesus. His letter to the early church reminded people of how much God loves them and how important it is to build a relationship with God.

DID YOU KNOW?

According to scholars, James's letter became a book of the Bible. It's named after him and is simply called James.

INDEX OF HEROES AND VILLAINS

ISBN: 978-1-945470-72-1

WorthyKids
Hachette Book Group
1290 Avenue of the Americas
New York, NY 10104

Published by WorthyKids, an imprint of Hachette Book Group, in association with Museum of the Bible.

museum of the Bible

BOOKS

Copyright © 2019 by Museum of the Bible, Inc.
409 3rd St. SW
Washington, D.C. 20024-4706
Museum of the Bible is an innovative, global, educational institution whose
purpose is to invite all people to engage with the history, narrative, and impact
of the Bible.

Illustrations by Pablo Pino
Produced with the assistance of Brentwood Studios, Franklin Tennessee

Cover photo: The History Collection/Alamy Stock Photo
Interior photos: 4 JoshuaDaniel/Shutterstock; 6 LittlePerfectStock/Shutterstock; 8 rafik beshay/
Shutterstock; 9 TheBiblePeople; Harvepino/Shutterstock; 10 DONOT6_STUDIO/Shutterstock;
12 Victor Jiang/Shutterstock; 14 SAPhotog/Shutterstock; 16 Guenter Albers/Shutterstock; 20 lullabi/
Shutterstock; 24 ruskpp/Shutterstock; 31 vvvita/Shutterstock; 40 Gino Santa Maria/Shutterstock;
53 Sopotnicki/Shutterstock; 56 Andrea Holien/www.pexels.com; 58 Krzysztof Slusarczyk/Shutterstock;
60 Nicku/Shutterstock; 67 Lebrecht Music & Arts/Alamy Stock Photo; 75 Ivan_off/Shutterstock;
76 vvvita/Shutterstock; 79 ArtMari/Shutterstock; 80 Alex Coan/Shutterstock; 85 TheBiblePeople;
86 Dimos/Shutterstock; 90 panda3800/Shutterstock; 92 Godong/Alamy Stock Photo; 94 Kai Beercrafter/
Shutterstock; 97 GoodWin777/Shutterstock; 101 Mauro Rodrigues/Shutterstock; 105 Bukhta Yurii/
Shutterstock; 107 Big Foot Productions/Shutterstock; 108 TheBiblePeople

Library of Congress CIP data on file

Printed and bound in the United States of America.
LSC-Craw_Jan19_1